THE SECRET LIFE OF POEMS

by the same author

poetry

A STATE OF JUSTICE
THE STRANGE MUSEUM
LIBERTY TREE
FIVEMILETOWN
SELECTED POEMS 1972–1990
WALKING A LINE
THE WIND DOG
THE INVASION HANDBOOK
THE ROAD TO INVER

adaptations

THE RIOT ACT: a version of Sophocles' *Antigone*
SEIZE THE FIRE: a version of Aeschylus' *Prometheus Bound*

play

THE HILLSBOROUGH SCRIPT: A Dramatic Satire

anthologies

THE FABER BOOK OF POLITICAL VERSE
THE FABER BOOK OF VERNACULAR VERSE
WILLIAM HAZLITT: The Fight and Other Writings (with David Chandler)
THOMAS HARDY (Poet-to-Poet series)
D. H. LAWRENCE (Poet-to-Poet series)

criticism

THOMAS HARDY: The Poetry of Perception
IRELAND AND THE ENGLISH CRISIS
MINOTAUR: Poetry and Nation State
WRITING TO THE MOMENT: Selected Critical Essays 1980–1996
THE DAY-STAR OF LIBERTY: Williams Hazlitt's Radical Style
CRUSOE'S SECRET: The Aesthetics of Dissent

TOM PAULIN

The Secret Life of Poems

A Poetry Primer

First published in 2008
by Faber and Faber Limited
3 Queen Square London WC1N 3AU

Typeset by Faber and Faber Ltd
Printed in England by Mackays of Chatham plc,
Chatham, Kent

A CIP record for this book
is available from the British Library

ISBN 978–0–571–22634–4

10 9 8 7 6 5 4 3 2 1

for Paul Muldoon

Contents

Metrical Feet

iamb	the day
pyrrhic	and a
spondee	blank street
trochee	tiger
anapaest	on the fold
dactyl	just for a
amphibrach	the forest
cretic	bang about
molossus	crust coarse-grained

Consonants

Aspirant: *h*
Fricative: *f*, *th*, *ph*
Dental (tongue and teeth): *d*, *n*, *s*, *t*
Guttural (throat and tongue): *g*, *k*
Labial (complete/partial lip closure): *p*, *b*, *f*, *v*, *w*
Liquid: *l*, *r*
Nasal (humming): *m*, *n*
Plosive: (strong) *p*, *t*, *k*; (weak) *b*, *d*, *g*
Sibilant (hissing): *s*, *sh*

THE SECRET LIFE OF POEMS: A POETRY PRIMER

Anonymous ~ 'The Unquiet Grave'

The wind doth blow today, my love,
And a few small drops of rain.
I never had but one true-love,
In cold grave she was lain.

I'll do as much for my true-love
As any young man may,
I'll sit and mourn all at her grave
For a twelvemonth and a day.

The twelvemonth and a day being up,
The dead began to speak:
Oh who sits weeping on my grave,
And will not let me sleep?

'Tis I, my love, sits on your grave,
And will not let you sleep,
For I crave one kiss of your clay-cold lips,
And that is all I seek.

You crave one kiss of my clay-cold lips,
But my breath smells earthy strong.
If you have one kiss of my clay-cold lips,
Your time will not be long.

'Tis down in yonder garden green,
Love, where we used to walk,
The finest flower that ere was seen
Is withered to a stalk.

The stalk is withered dry, my love,
So will our hearts decay.
So make yourself content, my love,
Till God calls you away.

Poetry begins in speech, in the skipping rhymes and chants children make up in the playground and the street. It moves from there into the imagination and life of the common people – into rhymes, riddles, traditional songs – and is then sometimes collected so that it moves from oral tradition, communal memory, into print. Because poetry is rooted in speech, in the common tongue, poets have turned to the energies of traditional song, as well as to nursery and skipping rhymes, to keep in touch with the genius of the language and to prevent their writing from becoming bookish and cloistered. Burns and Clare collected traditional songs and enjoyed their bawdiness, Wordsworth and Coleridge imitated traditional ballads, Christina Rossetti and Hopkins were fascinated by nursery and skipping rhymes. Rossetti published a volume of her own nursery rhymes – *Sing-Song* – and Hopkins said that what he called sprung rhythm is found in 'nursery rhymes, weather saws'. Writing to his friend R. W. Dixon, he explained it:

> I had long haunting my ear the echo of a new rhythm which now I realised on paper. To speak shortly, it consists in scanning by accents or stresses alone, without any account of the number of syllables, so that a foot may be one strong syllable or it may be many light and one strong. I do not say the idea is altogether new; there are hints of it in music, in nursery rhymes and popular jingles, in the poets themselves . . . Here are instances: *Díng, dóng, béll*; Pússy's ín the wéll. *Whó pút her ín?* Líttle Jóhnny Thín. *Whó púlled her óut?* Líttle Jóhnny Stóut.' For if each line has three stresses or feet it follows that some of the feet are of one syllable only.

That most hermetic and difficult of symbolist poets, Mallarmé, taught his school pupils English nursery rhymes – to the great anger of a school inspector in 1880, who was horrified that Mallarmé had his pupils chanting:

> Liar liar lick spit
> your tongue shall be split
> and all the dogs in the town
> shall have a little bit

This is nonsense, the inspector wrote, wondering if their teacher was a sick man. But Mallarmé was instilling in his pupils a knowledge of the deep rhythmic structures of a language, which differs from French in its love of the spontaneous vernacular.

Thomas Hardy, who was the son of a fiddler and stone mason, knew many traditional songs and draws on their rhythms, forms and subjects throughout his writing. He would have agreed with Hopkins's remark that Tennyson's 'Locksley Hall' is a 'wonderfully ingenious piece of versification, wonderfully faithful to the rule which the writer had evidently put before him, yet I grew utterly satiate and weary with it, on this very account. It had the effect of being artificial and *light*: most unfit for intense passion, of which indeed there is nothing in it, but only a man making an unpleasant and rather ungentlemanly row.' We can see an opposite effect in this famous Belfast street song :

> My aunt Jane has a bell on the door
> a white stone step and a clean swept floor
> candy apples hard green pears
> conversation lozengers
> candy apples hard green pears
> conversation lozengers

This is sprung rhythm, a rhythm that delights in now and then texturing what in metrics is known as a 'molossus' – three strong stresses – into the metre. So 'white stone step', 'clean swept floor' and 'hard green pears' confidently play against the anapaestic and trochaic rhythms that the lines establish.

Such songs are seldom studied, but there is something so uniquely and humanly beautiful about their cadences that no consideration of the nature of poetry can afford to ignore them. The first stanza of the ballad 'The Unquiet Grave' seems to echo these famous lines:

Westron wynde when wylle thow blow
the small rayne down can Rayne
Cryst yf my love were in my Armys
and I yn my bed Agayne

On the other hand, this late fifteenth-century lyric may be picking up 'The Unquiet Grave'. As in 'My aunt Jane' the stressy, natural rhythm packs three stresses together – 'the small rayne down'. The effect is tactile, indisputable, a hard fact of experience, which is both material and poignant, like tears hitting and biting. The west wind is hard and intimate – 'thow' which assonates immediately with 'blow', so that 'wynde' carries 'whine', 'grief', and then releases the rhyme with 'Cryst', like an oath, before impacting on 'I', and releasing another agony in 'Agayne', which takes all the stress of the previous *n*s. The 'bed' he desires is near to 'dead' and carries also the plosive in 'blow'. The urge to fold his dead love in his arms is countered by the image of Christ with outstretched arms.

The first stanza of 'The Unquiet Grave' reworks the lines, beginning with a perfect iambic tetrameter, then changing to a line which puts three stresses together and so changes the rhythm, making it more tactile and immediate, then switching back into iambic before putting four strong stresses together, then three in the next line. The next stanza builds a spondee ('true love') against a molossus ('young men may'), before repeating the molossus ('mourn all at') and returning to the spondee ('twelvemonth') and completing the stanza with a fluid anapaest ('and a day').

Out of the guttural in 'speak' and the softer guttural in 'grave', the next verse prepares the strong, disturbing, tantalising line : 'For I crave one kiss of your clay-cold lips', and then carries the guttural into 'clay-cold lips', whose three stresses echo the earlier triple, bunched stresses.

Then the dead woman's voice speaks back to him, making 'earthy' reflect 'breath', just as 'decay' in the last stanza brings 'clay' with it. Put an end to your grief, she says, or it will consume and destroy you. Let me go or you will kill your heart before it is time. Between that 'withered stalk' and the word from French 'content', something is going on – she is both a beautiful woman, the 'finest flower', and his shrivelled phallus, and also his obstinate memory of her body, her cunt, in 'content'. Let him remember them happily together before it is his turn to die. The 'garden green' is the bed they shared and made love in; 'walk' is that action and engagement – and it carries and transcends 'weeping' and 'sleep'. Her wise voice both cherishes and rebukes him, and in the mention of God, with its softer guttural, she gives him hope.

Sir Thomas Wyatt ~ 'They Fle from me that Sometyme Did me Seke'

They fle from me that sometyme did me seke
With naked fote stalking in my chambre.
I have sene theim gentill tame and meke
That nowe are wyld and do not remembre
That sometyme they put theimself in daunger
To take bred at my hand; and nowe they raunge
Besely seking with a continuell chaunge.

Thancked be fortune, it hath ben othrewise
Twenty tymes better; but ons in speciall
In thyn arraye after a pleasaunt gyse,
When her lose gowne from her shoulders did fall,
And she me caught in her armes long and small;
Therewithall swetely did me kysse,
And softely saide, *dere hert, howe like you this?*

It was no dreme: I lay brode waking.
But all is torned thorough my gentilnes
Into a straunge fasshion of forsaking;
And I have leve to goo of her goodenes,
And she also to vse new fangilnes.
But syns that I so kyndely ame serued,
I would fain knowe what she hath deserued.

Sir Thomas Wyatt was the foremost poet at the court of Henry VIII. He was reputedly the lover of Anne Boleyn, though most historians doubt this, and was imprisoned in the Tower of London along with her supposed lovers, whose executions he probably witnessed on 17 May 1536. He was released and prospered, but when his protector,

Thomas Cromwell, was executed on 28 July 1540, his life was again in danger. As he said in a poem about this event, Cromwell was his 'pillar' and was now 'perished'. Wyatt was charged with having encompassed the death of the king in a conversation in Rome with Cardinal Pole, Henry's enemy. But he was again released and died of a fever in 1542.

In a chalk drawing by Hans Holbein the Younger, Wyatt looks sideways, a tough but anxious courtier. Choosing a plain style in his most famous poem, he speaks directly, not in a courtier's voice, though he chooses a stanza form – rhyme royal – used by James I of Scotland and brought into English by Chaucer. 'They Fle from me', is often linked to Anne Boleyn, though the *Dictionary of National Biography* states that neither Wyatt's poetry nor his imprisonment have any connection with her.

The four long *ee* sounds begin a game of hide and seek in a perfect iambic pentameter; then in the next line the rhythm changes, as the guttural *k* at the end of 'seke' travels down to 'naked' and gives it prominence – a naked foot is stealthy, soundless, a naked blade is dangerous, a naked body attractive. The adjective almost vibrates with such suggestions, as well as describing his honest, thinking voice. The guttural, repeated in 'stalking', gives that verb even more prominence, as if each of his former lovers is on tiptoe. It's a hunting term, which means 'to steal up to game under cover', as well as to 'stride, walk in a stately or imposing manner'. It is an ugly word which suggests a powerful creature stealthily hunting a defenceless animal. Here, Wyatt feminises himself as the hart, which is the subject of so much love poetry. The verb is also prominent because it is a reversed iambic foot – 'stālkiˣng' – but as the next two feet – 'īn myˣ chāmbrˣe' – follow the same pattern, we could call these feet trochaic. The rhythm is tenser, tauter, more definite, compared with the relaxed iambic line that opens the poem.

This change in tone starts the sense of danger, and the next line continues the trochaic rhythm: 'Ī hˣave/ sēne thˣeim/ gēntˣill/ tāme/

and meke'. This, though, is a subtle line because we hear 'and meke' as a single unit, as an iambic foot, which picks up the first line and leads into the third, which begins with two iambic feet. This means that we hear 'tame' as a monosyllabic, stressed foot as the hunting metaphor continues, because Wyatt's courtly readers would have known that the term 'faucon gentil ' was applied to the female goshawk. Hopkins would probably have agreed that 'tame' is a single stressed foot.

The *ee* sounds in the first line are twice recalled in this line, so seeking and fleeing are part of its atmosphere, and slightly subvert the 'gentill tame and meke' adjectives that characterise the women as tame hawks or deer, and so restore the poet's masculine power, though 'me' can twice be discerned in the phrase. These women are 'gentill', a French word that means pleasant and well-mannered, as well as of a superior social class. The *ay* in 'tame' softens the *ay* in 'naked', while keeping the ghost of nudity somewhere in play. But the 'I' at the beginning of the third line foregrounds 'wyld' and makes it emphatic. From tame creatures that once ate bread from his hand, they now become like hawks that have turned wild, as tame hawks are prone to do. They range the skies 'seking' – a version of 'stalking', a repetition of 'seke' – for defenceless prey.

The dactyls and trochees that begin the last line of the first stanza – 'Besely seking with a' – speed up the movement after the drawn-out pause on 'raunge' (the pause is lengthened because of the rhyme back to 'daunger', a word which infects the free and powerful verb 'raunge').

Wyatt now takes up the *s* sounds at the start of the last line, and uses them in the next stanza to figure the erotic, ending the stanza on the sensuous *kiss/this*. But 'caught' brings back the *aw* – ugly sound – in 'stalking'. He is now caught up in the wheel of fortune – 'chaunge' leads naturally to 'fortune'. There is something uneasy in her arms being 'long and small' – maybe the rhyme demands it, but perhaps there's a spider in here somewhere? A long arm is a powerful arm, which contradicts the diminutive 'small'. The long *ees* in the first line – 'seke' especially – are brought into play by 'swetely', and repeated in 'dere' – punning on the animal – and 'dreme'.

Many lines, like the opening line of the third stanza, are divided by a strong caesura, because Wyatt's ear is still tuned to the alliterative rhythms of Middle English verse. The two *ays* in that line take us back to 'naked', and emphasise the change in power and circumstances since those times. This line also draws attention to itself, because it consists of only four feet, as does 'Into a straunge fasshion of forsaking'. She is active, he is passive, taking her gentleness onto himself, which causes her to reject him. He asks a mock-naive question at the end, a question which has a sinister quality in that he clearly knows what has happened to her. The *serued/deserued* rhyme is used by Chaucer in *Troilus and Criseyde*, and this points to the nature of their relationship (like Criseyde she has betrayed him). The three *i* sounds in the final couplet work to place great emphasis through contrast on 'she'. The effect is to target her, the object of his paranoid sexual fantasy, erotic memories and vindictive anger. The last couplet rather diminishes the poem – there is a mock courtesy in 'fain', but there is also implicitly 'pain'. This is the last of these long *ay* sounds.

George Herbert ~ 'The Flower'

How fresh, O Lord, how sweet and clean
Are thy returns! ev' n as the flowers in spring;
To which, besides their own demean,
The late-past frosts tributes of pleasure bring.
Grief melts away
Like snow in May,
As if there were no such cold thing.

Who would have thought my shrivel'd heart
Could have recover'd greennesse? It was gone
Quite under ground; as flowers depart
To see their mother-root, when they have blown;
Where they together
All the hard weather,
Dead to the world, keep house unknown.

These are thy wonders, Lord of power,
Killing and quickning, bringing down to hell
And up to heaven in an houre;
Making a chiming of a passing-bell.
We say amisse,
This or that is:
Thy word is all, if we could spell.

O that I once past changing were,
Fast in thy Paradise, where no flower can wither!
Many a spring I shoot up fair,
Offring at heav'n, growing and groning thither:
Nor doth my flower
Want a spring-showre,
My sinnes and I joining together.

But while I grow in a straight line,
Still upwards bent, as if heav'n were mine own,
Thy anger comes, and I decline:
What frost to that? what pole is not the zone,
Where all things burn,
When thou dost turn,
And the least frown of thine is shown?

And now in age I bud again,
After so many deaths I live and write;
I once more smell the dew and rain,
And relish versing: O my onely light,
It cannot be
That I am he
On whom thy tempests fell all night.

These are thy wonders, Lord of love,
To make us see we are but flowers that glide:
Which when we once can finde and prove,
Thou hast a garden for us, where to bide.
Who would be more,
Swelling through store,
Forfeit their Paradise by their pride.

I want to look at how rhythm works in the first stanza of Herbert's poem 'The Flower' and in the opening lines of one of Lawrence's finest poems, 'Bare Fig-Trees'.

The first stanza of 'The Flower' is the subtlest of all the stanzas in its cadence and rhythm. It can be taken as a model of the essentially redemptive nature of poetic rhythm. Poetry is not made up of image or of rich and complex language – it can be, but it does not have to possess these things.

Let us scan it:

> How fresh, O Lord, how sweet and clean
> Are thy returns! ev'n as the flowers in spring;
> To which, besides their own demean

These lines are almost completely regular iambic tetrameters, but the rhythm starts to shift:

> The late-past frosts tributes of pleasure bring

The spondee in the second foot textures and slows the line, then we get two short lines, each of two feet:

> Grief melts away
> Like snow in May

The first line is a spondee followed by an iamb, the next line is a straightforward iambic dimeter, which launches what we expect is another straightforward iambic line, which would scan:

> As if there were no such cold thing

If we read it in this way we get a jumpy, unnatural, rather daft-sounding line.

What happens is a kind of acoustic miracle: 'snow' triangulates with 'no' and with 'cold' to give each word great emphasis and to halt the line momentarily at 'no', before allowing it to go forward, to stop again ever so slightly at 'cold', which reverberates with two anterior *o* sounds impacting on its own *o*, before reaching 'thing'. The line has broken away from being composed of four iambic feet, and scans like this:

> As if/ there were no/ such cold thing

The first foot is an iamb, the next an anapaest, the third an anapaest which really wants to be a spondee if it could only shed that unstressed 'such'. Normally nouns take more stress than adjectives but 'cold' carries such weight, as I say, from the two previous *o* sounds that it perhaps even carries a shade more stress than 'thing'. Put together and launched by the short two previous lines, they sound meticulous and unchallengeable. This is how poetry works. As Robert Frost, said 'the ear does it'.

The redemptive nature of metre can also be found, curiously, in D. H. Lawrence, who mostly avoids traditional stress metre in his best poems, which are all in free verse. But if we look at the opening of 'Bare Fig-Trees' we can see another miracle of rhythm:

> Fig-trees, weird fig-trees
> Made of thick smooth silver,
> Made of sweet, untarnished silver in the sea-southern air –
> I say untarnished, but I mean opaque –

The poem begins heavily, straining for lift-off: 'Fig-trees, weird fig-trees' is a spondee, followed by a molossus, by three strong stresses. Every syllable is stressed, and the repetition boxes the line in. The next line consists of a trochee, 'Made of', followed by three strong stresses and an unstressed syllable: 'thick smooth silver'. Three adjectives in two short lines is risky, but he adds three or four, depending on how you count the compound adjective, in the next line: 'Made of sweet, untarnished silver in the sea-southern air'. Nine stresses, five *s* sounds, this line is struggling, and that compound adjective 'sea-southern' is an uncomfortable combination of 'sea air' and 'southern air', doubly so, because we don't talk about 'southern air'. Really this poem has failed to get off the ground.

Then in the next line, Lawrence makes it all suddenly run right, interjecting an afterthought between dashes:

> I say untarnished but I mean opaque –

This is a perfect iambic pentameter, which confesses to a mistake in the previous line. Lawrence's puritan aesthetic of spontaneity allows him to make mistakes, to work hit and miss, so that we see him like an artist in his studio having another stab at something he's just painted.

This means that when he returns to the bark of the fig trees, the adjectives are somehow cleansed of the effort of the first three lines.

> Thick, smooth-fleshed silver, dull only as human limbs are dull
> With the life-lustre,
> Nude with the dim light of full, healthy life
> That is always half-dark,
> And suave like passion-flower petals,
> Like passion-flowers,
> With the half-secret gleam of a passion-flower hanging from the rock,
> Great, complicated, nude fig-tree, stemless flower-mesh,
> Flowerily naked in flesh, and giving off hues of life.

The repeated *uh* sounds in 'dull', 'lustre', the run of *d* and *l* sounds, the chime of 'light' and 'life', the memory of 'silver' in 'suave', the plosives in 'passion' and 'petals', suddenly build a meshing pattern of related and relating sounds. He has succeeded in transforming metal into soft flesh. The word 'hues' in the last line of this, the first section of the poem carries 'smooth' in the second line to give the bark a living – a smooth but changing – complexion, which 'gives off' an inspired scent.

The *less/mesh/flesh* chime travels back to that repeated, highlighted word 'untarnished', just as 'naked' picks up 'opaque' – the sounds are like charged particles, constantly in motion, once they've been energised by the sudden interjection of the fourth line. This is dynamic form, picking itself up as it goes along.

John Donne ~ 'A Nocturnall upon St Lucies Day'

Tis the yeares midnight, and it is the dayes,
Lucies, who scarce seaven houres herself unmaskes,
  The Sunne is spent, and now his flasks
  Send forth light squibs, no constant rayes;
    The worlds whole sap is sunke:
The generall balme th'hydroptic earth hath drunk,
Whither, as to the beds-feet, life is shrunke,
Dead and enterr'd; yet all these seeme to laugh,
Compared with me, who am their Epitaph.

Study me then, you who shall lovers bee
At the next world, that is, at the next Spring:
  For I am every dead thing,
  In whom love wrought new Alchimie.
    For his art did expresse
A quintessence even from nothingnesse,
From dull privations, and leane emptinesse
He ruin'd me, and I am re-begot
Of absence, darknesse, death; things which are not.

All others, from all things, draw all that's good,
Life, soul, forme, spirit, whence they beeing have;
  I, by loves limbecke, am the grave
  Of all, that's nothing. Oft a flood
    Have wee two wept, and so
Drownd the whole world, us two; oft did we grow
To be two Chaosses, when we did show
Care to ought else; and often absences
Withdrewe our souls, and made us carcasses.

But I am by her death, (which word wrongs her)
Of the first nothing, the Elixer grown;
Were I a man, that I were one,
I needs must know; I should preferre,
If I were any beast,
Some ends, some means; Yea plants, yea stones detest,
And love; All, all some properties invest;
If I an ordinary nothing were,
As shadow, a light, and body must be here.

But I am none; nor will my Sunne renew.
You lovers, for whose sake, the lesser Sunne
At this time to the Goat is runne
To fetch new lust, and give it you,
Enjoy your summer all;
Since shee enjoyes her long nights festivall,
Let me prepare towards her, and let mee call
This hour her Vigil, and her Eve, since this
Both the yeares, and the dayes deep midnight is.

This study in negation begins dismissively – 'Tis the yeares midnight' – then it becomes more formal and paced, as the *ih* in 'Tis', repeated in 'mid', is then brought together by 'it is': *ih ih,* like two hard punches. The space between the two sounds is abolished. The compensation for this is the way the three strong stresses on 'yeares midnight' give way to the spaced out 'is the dayes'. This is perfectly natural, spontaneous, but carrying death and despondency in those repeated *d*s. This is only a preparation for the last line with its three *d*s and appearance of absolute finality.

After the first line the italicised '*Lucies*' comes as a relief, but Donne's ear runs away with the double *s* sound and he repeats the sound again and again, an uneasy and anxious susurrus. In the next line, Donne continues to flog the *s* sound. It is as if the sun has ejaculated, and is only weakly capable of sending forth light. The stars store light as flasks store gunpowder, and there may be a pun on 'flashes'. His ear has also got attracted to the guttural *k* in 'unmaskes', and it runs through 'squibs', 'sunke', 'hydroptique', 'shrunke'. Partly 'hydroptique' draws attention to itself, because it doesn't combine *k* with a sibilance, but also because it is trisyllabic and technical, diagnostic, and he has been deliberately placing simple monosyllables in the middle of the line before the caesura – *spent squibs sap*. Donne elides the repeated definite article to place the harsh, dry, technical 'th'hydroptique' in the middle of the line – a broken-backed, compound word with the caesura concealed inside it. The word sounds nasty and contains 'drop', i.e. fall. The *ds* come back here putting strong emphasis on 'drunk', which reverberates in the *unk unk unk* rhyme. The crisp plosives in 'spent' and 'sap' are emphasised in the 'drop' in 'hydroptique' – and the descent continues in 'beds-feet'; then the plosives recur in 'Compar'd' and 'Epitaph', where the second *p* is not heard as the couplet completes itself.

The dental *ds* give strength to the three opening lines of the next stanza, but Donne again wants to challenge his monosyllables with the technical 'Alchimie' followed by 'quintessence', 'nothingnesse', 'privations'. When he introduces another technical term in 'limbecke' in the next stanza, he picks up 'hydroptique' and sets up 'Chaosses' and 'carcasses'. That last word rubs out the run of *ws*, which begins with 'wee two wept'.

This sequence is picked up by 'which word wrongs her' – the voice drops here because the clause is held within brackets, so it seems to stand out from the rhythm of the poem. But the four strong stresses are doubled in:

Sōme ēnds, sōme mēans; Yēa plānts, yēa stōnes dĕtēst

There are nine stresses here, and their spondaic weight is repeated in 'All, all', which varies the double stress by putting the caesura in between the stresses, and making this moment vocal, anguished, as he bears witness with that repeated 'yea'.

In the last stanza, the repeated *uh* links 'None' and 'Sunne', conflating them, so that 'None' negates 'lovers', 'Sunne', 'runne', 'lust' and 'summer'. The last line is even more negative than the first, but there is a strange softness in its cadence, which slows the line and gives a type of contemplative wonder to it. This is because 'Eve' becomes prominent because it repeats the *v* in 'Vigill' and carries the long *ee* in 'mee' before handing it on to 'yeares' and 'deep'. We rest on 'deep' so completely that the poem seems to want to end there. The last two words are almost like an afterthought. This is similar to the casual 'Tis the yeares midnight' – it is a vocal, spontaneous, and at the end a falling cadence. At almost the last moment, 'deep' becomes the poem's high point – nothing can equal it: it does not take us down to the 'beds-feet' but up towards the sun and the stars. It does not exist in that first line, so it is unforeseen, not a repetition. In this word 'me', 'yeares' and 'her Eve' are united in love and rebegotten – but hardly so we notice it, though faintly there's a trace of Eve. His emphasis on 'new lust' and 'enjoyes' in the last stanza should alert us to what he means by 'deep', but it's a forlorn hope, a forlorn desire. The poem ends with five strong stresses, with a particular stress on 'is' as he picks up 'Tis' and 'is' from the first line.

William Shakespeare ~ Sonnet 73

That time of yeeare thou maist in me behold
When yellow leaues, or none, or few, doe hange
Vpon those boughes which shake against the could,
Bare ruin'd qiers, where late the sweet birds sang.
In me thou seest the twi-light of such day,
As after Sun-set fadeth in the West,
Which by and by blacke night doth take away,
Deaths second self that seals vp all in rest.
In me thou seest the glowing of such fire,
That on the ashes of his youth doth lye,
As the death bed, whereon it must expire,
Consum'd with that which it was nurrisht by.
This thou perceu'st, which makes thy loue more strong,
To loue that well which thou must leaue ere long.

In 1930, William Empson published a seminal work of literary criticism, *Seven Types of Ambiguity*. He wrote it on a portable typewriter while he was an undergraduate at Cambridge, and in discussing Sonnet 73 he offered this terse aside:

> There is no pun, double syntax, or dubiety of feeling in 'Bare ruined choirs, where late the sweet birds sang', but the comparison holds for many reasons, because ruined monastery choirs are places in which to sing, because they involve sitting in a row, because they are made of wood, are carved into knots and so forth, because they used to be surrounded by a sheltering building crystallised out of the likeness of a forest, and coloured with stained glass and painting like flowers and leaves, because they are now abandoned by all but the grey walls coloured like the skies of winter, because the cold and Narcissistic charm suggested by choir-boys suits well with Shakespeare's feeling for the object of the

> Sonnets, and for various sociological and historical reasons (the Protestant destruction of monasteries; fear of Puritanism),which it would be hard now to trace out in their proportions; these reasons, and many more relating the simile to its place in the Sonnet, must all combine to give the line its beauty, and there is a sort of ambiguity in not knowing which of them to hold most clearly in mind. Clearly this is involved in all such richness and heightening of effect, and the machinations of ambiguity are among the very roots of poetry.

The ambiguity he is pointing to is historical, and at that time highly political because it carries sympathy for the practices and architecture of the old religion, Catholicism. Eventually, many years later, Empson's remark was to bear fruit in Ted Hughes's enormous study of Shakespeare, *The Goddess of Complete Being,* and in many scholarly discussions as to whether Shakespeare was a Catholic.

An ambiguity, Empson states, means something 'very pronounced, and as a rule witty or deceitful'. It gives room for 'alternative reactions' to the same piece of language. The joy of ambiguity is that it empowers the reader to find subtleties in a text, which open out like a secret labyrinth below the printed words. To adapt Eliot's lines on the Treaty of Versailles, poems are revealed to have 'many cunning passages, contrived corridors/ And issues'. Tracing what Empson in a revealing phrase terms 'the machinations of ambiguity', we enter the intricate, devious world of the imagination with its multiple ironies, its trembling light and fluid playfulness.

Shakespeare is talking about what it feels like to be middle-aged and unloved, when he compares himself to a tree in autumn. Lonely and fearing death, he is like the 'boughes' of a tree, which shake against the 'could'. The word 'could', pronounced as it often is in the north of Ireland, where Elizabethan pronunciation and some of its vocabulary are still current, picks up 'boughs' and makes the *ow* sound stronger, sadder. We remember that poor Tom in *Lear* is 'acould'. And in 'bare' we remember that 'poor, bare, forked animal' in *Lear.*

But then Shakespeare offers a metaphor for the boughs, and we see them as empty, bare choir stalls, which have been broken up and thrown out of a church. This had happened two generations ago, so this is a moment of Catholic antiquarianism. The Elizabethan injunctions of 1559 enjoined clergy to 'take away, utterly extinct and destroy all shrines, covering of shrines, all tables and candlesticks, trundles or rolls of ware, pictures, paintings and all other monuments of feigned miracles, pilgrimages, idolatry and superstition, *so that there remain no memory of the same* in walls, glasses, windows or elsewhere within their churches or houses'. Also the *hange/sang* rhyme maybe an echo of Psalm 137 ('we hanged up our harps'), which gives the rhyme an exilic and therefore Catholic association.

Shakespeare's father, John, who was a devout Catholic, had to preside over this destruction of the altars – he appears to have cooperated with the authorities slowly and reluctantly. The word 'late' means 'in the recent past', and it refers to the dissolution of the monasteries and the stripping of the altars by an aggressive iconoclastic Protestantism. The *t* in 'late' touches the *t* in 'sweet', an obsessive adjective in the sonnets, where it sometimes has a type of camp inflection, like Falstaff calling Prince Hal 'sweet boy'. As Empson points out, the narcissism here seems appropriate for choir boys.

Within the historical image, Shakespeare is also offering a Catholic image of the crucifixion. His flesh hangs on his skeleton like dead leaves or like Christ's body on the cross – the images of body/tree, body/cross, body/church are perfectly fused. Shakespeare plays on *leaues loue leaue,* as he tries to make the narcissistic, selfish young man he is in love with realise both his own mortality and the poet's and so return his love – a hopeless argument. The agony of being hopelessly in love becomes a cry out of the English Catholic experience of martyrdom and persecution (the head of Shakespeare's mother's family, Edward Arden, was executed as a traitor because he was a Catholic).

What Empson is pointing to is how we cannot draw a distinction between personal experience – being in love – and lived historical experience. The combination of the word 'hange' and 'shake' means that 'upon' could refer to the scaffold where so many Catholics were executed at Tyburn and elsewhere. Cruelly, Shakespeare rhymes 'sang' with 'hange', and so introduces a sinister sound to what should be a simply joyous verb. In a sense, he ruins the rhyme too.

In her epic study of the sonnets, Helen Vendler identifies a key-word which occurs in each quatrain, and a couplet tie, a word or words, which appear in the body of the sonnet and are then repeated in the couplet. The couplet tie in this sonnet is *leaue*[*s*], but she does not identify a key-word. In my view, there is a key long vowel sound *ee*, which appears several times in each quatrain, and is then repeated twice in the couplet. This binds the sonnet together, and gives great emphasis to the almost last word, 'leaue'.

Vendler sees 'glowing' as a 'positive word', but it could be argued that that noun, which she sees as no longer a noun 'but rather a verbal, an action', and therefore 'a glowing, not a dying', picks up 'yellow', which casts a shadow over it, just as 'hangs' crosses 'sang'. Rather, I think, this is an image of the unnaturally glowing complexion of a dying person – the 'bloom', in Keats's 'To Autumn', on the 'soft-dying day'.

Shakespeare is characterising himself as feeling similar to bits of holy furniture, which have been chucked like so much rubbish onto a bonfire. The Elizabethans spelt and pronounced that word 'bone-fire', a pronunciation that survives in the north of Ireland to this day. So the boughs are choir stalls and bones – we are close to the idea of martyrdom here, as a metaphor for dying lonely and loveless. Those hanging yellow leaves begin this idea, for this is a poem written in a consistent code. Just as Pasternak's 'Hamlet in Russia' is coded for the dilemma of artists under Stalin, this sonnet is coded for Elizabeth or James's regime, depending where one dates the sonnets. Shakespeare's multi-layered, shifting, ambiguous language reflects the dilemma of the Catholic artist in a harshly Protestant state.

William Shakespeare ~ from *Macbeth*

Enter Macbeth, Lennox and Ross.

Had I but died an hour before this chance,
I had lived a blessèd time; for from this instant
There's nothing serious in mortality:
All is but toys. Renown and grace is dead,
The wine of life is drawn and the mere lees
Is left this vault to brag of.

Enter Malcolm and Donalbain. [II.iii.91–6]

The third scene of Act Two begins with the porter's speech as we hear the knocking on the gate. The knocking begins near the end of the previous scene, just after Lady Macbeth has gone backstage to gild the faces of the murdered grooms with their blood. Macbeth is on his own, and the heavy, repeated sound becomes a physical symbol of his disturbed conscience:

Whence is that knocking?
How is't with me, when every noise appalls me?
What hands are here? Ha! They pluck out mine eyes!
Will great Neptune's ocean wash this blood
Clean from my hand? No; this my hand will rather
The multitudinous seas incarnadine
Making the green one red.

Lady Macbeth enters and rebukes him: 'A little water clears us of this deed'. But the knocking continues, and the scene closes with Macbeth's couplet:

> To know my deed, 'twere best not know myself.
> (*Knock*)
> Wake Duncan, with thy knocking! I would thou could'st.

Macbeth has earlier called his bloody hands 'hangman's hands' – meaning they look as though they have drawn the bowels and plucked the heart out of the body of a half-hanged man, who was usually a traitor, as Macbeth now is. This was the fate of John Grant, the conspirator in the Gunpowder Plot, whom Shakespeare is most likely to have known. The word 'drawn' in 'the wine of life is drawn' carries somewhere a memory of 'hung, drawn and quartered'. Macbeth's speech is disturbed, guilty, full of regret for what he has done; he speaks mostly in short phrases, with only one full pentameter: 'The labour we delight in physics pain', his glib, civil answer to Macduff's politesse earlier in this scene (Macduff says he knows it is a 'joyful trouble' for Macbeth to bring him to Duncan). The word 'trouble' has already been used by Duncan, who when Lady Macbeth advances to welcome him into the castle, where he will be murdered, says to Banquo:

> See, see, our honoured hostess!
> The love that follows us sometime is our trouble,
> Which still we thank as love.

That word 'trouble' we hear three times in 'hubble, bubble, toil and trouble'. Shakespeare's characters use language as though they're unwittingly walking on eggshells, and in doing so they sow unease and attention in the audience.

When Duncan's murder is revealed, Macbeth gives the short speech that begins 'Had I but died an hour' – it is a speech made in public, but it sounds like one of Macbeth's earlier, agonised soliloquies. In Shakespeare's memory is Faustus's great final soliloquy, which he had earlier tried to imitate in Richard III's final speech before Bosworth Field:

> Give me another horse! Bind up my wounds!
> Have mercy, Jesu! Soft! I did but dream.
> O cursed conscience, how dost thou afflict me!
> The lights burn blue. It is now dead midnight.
> Cold fearful drops stand on my trembling flesh.

This speech protests too much. Now, remembering Marlowe's seminal, unprecedented soliloquy he takes the first line: 'Ah, Faustus, now hast thou but one bare hower to live', and puts the hour before, not after the present moment. That drawn-out, bisyllabic word (spelt 'houre' in the First Folio) also looks forward to one of his most tortured, later speeches:

> I have lived long enough. My way of life
> Is fall'n into the sear, the yellow leaf,
> And that which should accompany old age,
> As honour, love, obedience, troops of friends,
> I must not look to have.

When Macbeth says if he had lived an hour before this time he had lived a blessed time, his speech, with its *lived life lees left* anticipates the *lived life leaf love* pattern of the later speech, with its emphasis on unfulfilled time. The feudal order represented by 'Renown and grace' is spelt out by 'honour, love, obedience, troops of friends' – both represent the divinely ordained, hierarchical structure of the universe, which he has offended against.

Macbeth, testing Macduff, says that he does not possess 'the King-becoming graces', and then lists them:

> As justice, verity, temp'rance, stableness,
> Bounty, perseverance, mercy, lowliness,
> Devotion, patience, courage, fortitude.

Macbeth, with typical terseness, eloquently offers this clumsy list, and makes these virtues heart-felt and impossible for him to grasp and practise.

The word 'toys' takes emphasis – dismissive emphasis – because it echoes the *t* at the end of 'but', and then reverberates with 'lees' – both mushy, trivial – as well as suggesting the empty noise of 'brag'. It replies to 'serious' in the line before, denying its existence with a trivial monosyllable. The actor would need to spit the word out, then leave a pause before the next stately and religious nouns.

The power of this short speech derives from its brevity and sincerity. When, a few lines later, Macbeth embarks on a longer speech to explain why he killed the grooms, his rhetorical questions start to sound hollow, and Lady Macbeth faints to draw attention away from him and to shut him up. The line, 'His silver skin laced wi' his golden blood', is too rhetorical, though the next line – 'And his gashed stabs looked like a breach in nature' – carries both the physical act and the crime against the metaphorical structure of the universe. The word 'blessèd' speaks for the idea of holiness that suffuses this metaphorical structure. Its bisyllabic emphasis, like that on 'hour', speaks for an eternal holiness he is forever cast out from. It is a feudal, Catholic idea of the sacred, and it is embodied in both Duncan and the English king, Edward the Confessor. This sanctification of Duncan is one of the most significant reworkings of the original story. It's there too in 'the milk of human kindness', which Lady Macbeth says her husband has too much of. That phrase is varied in 'the wine of life', just as 'this vault' picks up Macbeth's earlier soliloquy in which he imagines how Duncan's virtues

> Will plead like angels trumpet-tongued against
> The deep damnation of his taking-off;
> And pity, like a naked new-born babe,
> Striding the blast, or heaven's cherubim horsed
> Upon the sightless couriers of the air,
> Shall blow the horrid deed in every eye,
> That tears shall drown the wind. I have no spur
> To prick the sides of my intent, but only

> Vaulting ambition, which o'erleaps itself
> And falls on th'other.

The word 'vault', which means cellar and grave and sky, also carries ambition with it. Partly Shakespeare is thinking of his own ambition as a poet, which is to vault beyond Marlowe, the great over-reacher. The wind blows, he implies, the horrid deed like dust in everyone's eyes, and the phrase 'mere lees' is a version of this image. Nothing sacred remains, he is left with the dregs.

The Shakespeare scholar Clare Asquith has shown that Shakespeare was also thinking of the vault under the House of Commons where Guy Fawkes and his fellow conspirators placed the barrels of gunpowder. There were contemporary references to 'the Devil in the Vault', and the great preacher Lancelot Andrewes said, 'In darkness they delighted, dark vaults, dark cellars and darkness fell upon them for it.' The play is suffused with allusions to the plot, which was discovered in the winter of 1605, a few months before the play was, it is thought, first performed at court.

In the speech, 'drawn' takes extra stress because it echoes 'dead'. The monosyllabic noun looks forward to a phrase Lady Macbeth uses in the banquet scene, when she tells Macbeth that his fear is 'the air-drawn dagger', which he told her led him to Duncan. The word 'drawn' therefore holds an association for Macbeth with 'dagger' – the dagger is first drawn on the air by his imagination, then he draws it from its scabbard to stab Duncan. What Macbeth is facing is his own loneliness in a dead universe – there is a sense of hollowness which 'brag' underlines. That ugly, apparently Anglo-Saxon word implies that he is a braggart, a hollow boaster (the word 'brag' actually comes from French *bragarder*, but that word comes from the Old Norse *brak*, which means 'creaking noise', so it's fair to see it as a North European word). Disturbed by his conscience, Macbeth sounds as though he is writing his own epitaph, until the several words from Latin and French – *chance blessed time instant serious mortality renown grace wine vault* – are undercut by that lumpish *brag*, a word he uses in Sonnet 18: 'Nor shall Death brag thou wand'rst in his shade', where it is again an ugly, resonant verb.

John Bunyan ~ 'Who Would True Valour See'

Who would true valour see
Let him come hither;
One here will constant be,
Come wind, come weather.
There's no discouragement,
Shall make him once relent,
His first avow'd intent,
To be a pilgrim.

Who so beset him round,
With dismal stories,
Do but themselves confound;
His strength the more is.
No lion can him fright,
He'll with a giant fight,
But he will have a right,
To be a pilgrim.

Hobgoblin, nor foul fiend,
Can daunt his spirit:
He knows, he at the end,
Shall life inherit.
Then fancies fly away,
He'll fear not what men say,
He'll labour night and day,
To be a pilgrim.

Near the end of the second part of *The Pilgrim's Progress*, Valiant describes his pilgrimage and sings a song that is one of the finest

English hymns. We think of hymns as straightforward vehicles of faith which unite congregations as they, for example, triumphantly sing 'Onward Christian Soldiers' to a marked and obvious tune, but 'Who Would True Valour See' is altogether more interesting. It is a simple and austere puritan lyric, but one that draws on Shakespeare, traditional song, Catholic as well as puritan experience of persecution, torture and martyrdom, and also on the Greenwood, one of the imaginative sources of the English idea of liberty and free speech.

In *As You Like It*, Amiens sings:

> Under the greenwood tree
>   Who loves to lie with me,
> And turn his merry note,
>   Unto the sweet bird's throat,
> Come hither, come hither, come hither.
>   Here shall I see no enemy
> But winter and rough weather.

Then Amiens, Jacques and the others sing:

> Who doth ambition shun
>   And loves to lie i th' sun,
> Seeking the food he eats,
>   And pleased with what he gets,
> Come, hither, come hither, come hither.
>   Here shall he see no enemy
> But winter and rough weather.

Bunyan sets his lines to a different tune, and he changes the rhyme scheme, but Shakespeare's 'come hither', and 'winter and rough weather' prompt him to shape his song. From the Forest of Arden to Bunyan's Bedfordshire there is a continuity of traditional song and popular culture which Bunyan draws on throughout *The Pilgrim's Progress*, where his ear for common speech and his study of the

Bible create some of the greatest prose in the language. In Valiant's song, his ear runs with a series of pinched *ih* sounds – *hither will him intent pilgrim*. The first five strengthen and toughen the spondee *pīlgrīm* to make it resonate and glow with conviction. Also the refrain drops a foot, so that it becomes simpler, tenser, firmer. The triple *ccc* rhyme also tightens each stanza – these are what used to be called 'masculine' rhymes – and they have a strong presence after the previous 'feminine' rhyme. They lock the lines in before the refrain frees the stanza.

By making the second line of the second stanza carry only two stresses (its equivalent in the first stanza has three), Bunyan isolates 'stories' and gives it an ironic emphasis that lowers both the stories and those who tell them. And by repeating the *st* in 'strength', he converts the syllable into a strong-standing gesture that echoes 'constant' in the first stanza. Here, Valiant is putting into noble and assured song the substance of a speech he made to a character called Greath, where he describes how his parents tried to make him stay at home:

> They told me of the Slow of *Dispond*, where *Christian* was well nigh Smothered. They told me that there were Archers standing ready in *Belzebub-Castle*, to shoot them that should knock at the *Wicket* Gate for Entrance. They told me also of the Wood, and dark Mountains, of the Hill *Difficulty*, of the Lyons, and also of the three *Gyants*, Bloodyman, *Maul*, and *Slay-good*. They said moreover, that there was a foul *Fiend* haunted the Valley of *Humiliation*, and that *Christian* was, by him, almost bereft of Life. Besides, said they, you must go over *the Valley of the Shadow of Death*, where the *Hobgoblins* are, where the Light is Darkness, where the Way is full of Snares, Pits, Traps and Ginns.

The landscape is partly taken from the heath in *King Lear*. There Shakespeare imagines the sufferings of English Catholics under the new Protestant and mercantilist forces embodied in the bastard, Edmund. His brother, Edgar, disguised as Poor Tom, hisses 'beware the foul fiend'. Shakespeare's mind is wedded to the feudal idea of hierarchy and duty, but Bunyan gives pitch and emphasis to 'right', a radical, political term, as he confronts the state – the giant – that had imprisoned him for seventeen years for preaching without permission. This was the Stuart regime, which persecuted Dissenters – 8,000 prisoners for their faith died of gaol fever – and which was to be overthrown by William of Orange in 1688, just after Bunyan's death.

In the second stanza, 'be' in the refrain takes on an extra, vibrating stress because it picks up 'he' in the previous line. Then we plunge into the Valley of the Shadow of Death, which is first described in the original *Pilgrim's Progress*, when Christian meets two men who have decided not to travel through the valley. Christian asks them what they have seen:

> Seen! Why the Valley itself, which is as dark as pitch; we also saw there the Hobgoblins, Satyrs, and Dragons of the Pit: we heard also in that Valley a continual howling and yelling, as of a people under unutterable misery; who there sat bound in affliction and Irons: and over that Valley hangs the discouraging Clouds of Confusion, death also doth always spread his wings over it: in a word, it is every whit dreadful, being utterly without Order.

This is a dissident's vision of Stuart persecution – Bunyan's prose, like Valiant's song, puts the sufferings of the Dissenters into a religious code to expose the lack of order in the state. Christian sees a cave where 'two Giants, *Pope* and *Pagan*, dwelt in old time, by whose power and Tyranny the Men whose bones, blood, ashes &c lay there, were cruelly put to death'. Here, that deadpan phrase 'old time' places the two giants back in a period before the Reformation, though Bunyan means his readers to identify the giants as Charles II and his cruel brother, James, Duke of York.

This land is cruel and alien, but the verb 'inherit', whose object is normally property, land, goods, points to the hope that Valiant and his people will one day enter into their rightful inheritance, when the meek shall inherit the earth. On the surface of the lyric, 'life' simply means eternal life in heaven, but that is code for an England free of laws that forbid Dissenters to worship God as they see fit. Out of 'life' four words containing *l* – *fly He'll He'll pilgrim* – take firm emphasis until Bunyan returns to another word beginning with *l* to assert the winning of that life. His confidence shows in the way he doesn't write the more polite or standard line 'he knows that at the end' because it would contain a slightly tacky middle rhyme – 'that at'. Instead, he designs a more spoken, more uplifting line whose repeated 'he' proudly affirms his belief and purpose. This short, beautiful lyric is packed with great historical and personal suffering – and with unyielding courage and conviction.

John Milton ~ from *Paradise Lost*

Hail holy light, offspring of heaven first-born,
Or of the eternal co-eternal beam
May I express thee unblamed? since God is light,
And never but in unapproachèd light
Dwelt from eternity, dwelt then in thee,
Bright effluence of bright essence increate.
Or hear'st thou rather pure ethereal stream,
Whose fountain who shall tell? before the sun,
Before the heavens thou wert, and at the voice
Of God, as with a mantle didst invest
The rising world of waters dark and deep,
Won from the void and formless infinite.
Thee I revisit now with bolder wing,
Escaped the Stygian pool, though long detained
In that obscure sojourn, while in my flight
Through utter and through middle darkness borne
With other notes than to the Orphean lyre
I sung of Chaos and eternal Night,
Taught by the heavenly Muse to venture down
The dark descent, and up to reascend,
Though hard and rare: thee I revisit safe,
And feel thy sovereign vital lamp; but thou
Revisit'st not these eyes, that roll in vain
To find thy piercing ray, and find no dawn;
So thick a drop serene hath quenched their orbs,
Or dim suffusion veiled. Yet not the more
Cease I to wander where the muses haunt
Clear spring, or shady grove, or sunny hill,
Smit with the love of sacred song; but chief

Thee Sion and the flowery brooks beneath
That wash thy hallowed feet, and warbling flow,
Nightly I visit: nor sometimes forget
Those other two equalled with me in fate,
So were I equalled with them in renown,
Blind Thamyris, and blind Maeonides,
And Tiresias and Phineus prophets old.
Then feed on thoughts, that voluntary move
Harmonious numbers; as the wakeful bird
Sings darkling, and in shadiest covert hid
Tunes her nocturnal note. Thus with the year
Seasons return, but not to me returns
Day, or the sweet approach of even or morn,
Or sight of vernal bloom, or summer's rose,
Or flocks, or herds, or human face divine;
But cloud instead, and ever-during dark
Surrounds me, from the cheerful ways of men
Cut off, and for the book of knowledge fair
Presented with a universal blank
Of nature's works to me expunged and razed,
And wisdom at one entrance quite shut out.
So much the rather thou celestial light
Shine inward, and the mind through all her powers
Irradiate, there plant eyes, all mist from thence
Purge and disperse, that I may see and tell
Of things invisible to mortal sight.

[Book 3, ll 1–55]

Book Two ends with Satan, 'fraught with mischievous revenge', heading towards earth. Now Milton opens the next book with an invocation to light. The alliterating *h*s in the first line build 'holy light' strongly, but almost immediately there is a problem, because it is conventional to hesitate at the opening of ancient hymns, and also because the first line is so arresting and sublime the verse cannot go any higher. It is struggling for lift-off, as 'off' in 'offspring' is caught up by 'of', and dragged down by the second 'of'. There is a similar effect in line 15 where the *f* in 'flight' snags the *l*.

The third line sounds a note of almost donnish, fussy hesitation, which follows from the alternative phrase 'eternal co-eternal beam', which he has just offered. It sounds slightly technical, a piece of jargon, but Milton picks himself up, and the verse rises magnificently, arresting its flow with a short couplet within one line – 'Dwelt from eternity,/ dwelt then in thee' – which almost gnomically appears to express the Trinity through those repeated *ee* sounds that might be ghosting 'three'. Milton, who didn't believe in a trinal triplicity, is making sure he doesn't mention that central theological concept.

He uses repetition again in the next line, which sounds good initially but on inspection seems like theological waffle. Here, he is drawing on William Drummond's 'An Hymn of the Fairest Fair', a strained address to the Trinity:

> O most holy One!
> Unprocreate Father, ever-procreate Son,
> Ghost breathed from both, you were, are, aye, shall be,
> Most blessed, three in one, and one in thee,
> Incomprehensible by reachless height,
> And unperceived by excessive light . . . so is the spring,
> The well-head, and the stream which they forth bring,
> Are but one selfsame essence, nor in aught
> Do differ, save in order, and our thought
> No chime of time discerns in them to fall,
> But three distinctly sire one essence all.

Milton telescopes Drummond's pious lines into a thuddingly alliterative line that ends with the ugly, technical adjective 'increate', whose *ee* sound is damagingly repeated four times in the next line, and which parodies a belief in threeness. The *beam/blame* play also casts a shadow over that *ee* sound

Milton is hesitating between a theological belief called Athanasianism, which asserts that Christ is consubstantial with the Father, and Arianism, which states that Christ is a lesser figure. He is hesitating because although he is by inclination an Arian, he knows that it is a capital offence to proclaim that doctrine. John Biddle, the father of English Unitarianism, was sentenced to death for his Arian beliefs, but Milton saved his life (Biddle was exiled to the Scilly Islands). So these opening lines are uneasy, coded, evasive, as Milton asks the God of light if he would prefer to be called 'pure ethereal stream', again a prefabricated phrase like 'bright essence increate.'

Milton has begun at a great height then plunged down for six lines – now with a question he begins to climb back. The *n* sound in the word 'fountain' refreshingly begets 'sun', and those repeated *ws* in 'world' and 'waters' culminate in 'Won', which stands at the beginning of the next line with its *w* in upper case to challenge 'lost' in the title of the epic and look forward to a victory beyond the temporary darkness of the unstable Stuart regime. Now Milton reprises God's creation of the world, and hints at his increased self-confidence after his imprisonment and the risk of severe punishment in the early months of the Restoration. Marvell picks up on this line in the opening line of his poem, 'On *Paradise Lost*', which was printed as an epigraph to the 1674 edition of the poem: 'When I beheld the poet blind, yet bold/ In slender book his vast design unfold'. The adjective 'bold' is a Whiggish term, which means 'innovative and risk-taking'.

Milton means that he has now moved his narrative from hell and chaos to earth, but the phrase 'bolder wing' sets up a parallel between his actions and Satan's, because early in the first book Satan speaks in 'bold words', and the adjective is often given to the fallen angels. Again, as I've suggested, he's glancing at his imprisonment after the Restoration in 'detained', and he would also have known that his many enemies would have regarded him as a satanic rebel. As well as this, he has an anxiety that he is guilty of a satanic pride in choosing to write an epic poem to rival all other epic poems.

He distinguishes himself from Orpheus, who descended into hell to recover Eurydice with the music of his lyre, but here, though these are very confident lines, he again introduces a deep anxiety that accompanied his experience of prison. He confronts that anxiety in Book Seven, where he invokes Urania and asks her to

> drive far off the barbarous dissonance
> Of Bacchus and his revellers, the race
> Of that wild rout that tore the Thracian bard
> In Rhodope.

The executed regicides were hanged, drawn and quartered on the scaffold, their hearts ripped by the executioner from their still living, conscious bodies. This is the fate Milton must have expected, and which some of his enemies hoped he would suffer. Again, the classical allusion is a coded reference to his deepest anxieties – the entire epic is coded as an account of the English revolution from the creation of the world/Commonwealth to the fall into monarchy. It is a systematic code that passed many inattentive, ahistorical or narrowly religious readers by, and probably still does.

From 'God' in line 10, the *d*s are strong and resolved in this passage, and so are the *t*s, both dentals aiding and reinforcing each other. We arrive at the phrase 'hard and rare' with emphasis in line 21, and also with a sense of recognition because this is an echo of this passage from near the end of Book Two:

> so eagerly the fiend
> O'er bog or steep, through strait, rough, dense or rare,

With head, hands, wings or feet pursues his way,
And swims or sinks, or wades, or creeps, or flies.

Milton has already used the adjective 'hard' earlier in Book Two, again in a satanic context: 'long is the way/ And hard, that out of hell leads up to light'. And Satan then talks of 'our prison strong' – he, like Milton, is detained in darkness.

Milton's imagination occupies dangerous territory – as a leading republican intellectual and polemical writer who served the Commonwealth, he has lived through the violence, the upsets, the 'barbarous dissonance', as he called it, of his age. Like the blind Oedipus, he can feel the sun on his sightless eyes. Those eyes 'roll in vain' to catch the light, and here he again echoes Satan and the fallen angels, whose 'eyes aghast/ Viewed first their lamentable lot, and found/ No rest' (2. 616–18). He then describes the eye disease that has robbed him of his sight. This is a low point, but a brief one, because in a characteristically hoisting upward movement, he introduces a beautiful pastoral passage filled with his love of the psalms. Those singing lines ring with an assured faith and a solidarity with Thamyris, Homer, Tiresias and Phineus. He is no longer alone and is following his epic mission with a confident resolve. He composes at night, like the nightingale singing in the dark. The gutturals in 'wakeful' and 'dazzling' texture the sound with a certain roughness. A note in my edition says that 'darkling' is 'not yet poetic'. In fact, it is the reverse of poetic in the context from which Milton took it:

For you know, nuncle,
The hedge-sparrow fed the cuckoo so long
That it had it head bit off by it young
So out went the candle, and we were left darkling.

The word 'darkling' is instinct with tragedy, though it also suggests 'darling' – 'little dear'. Its darkness is also the darkness of belonging to a powerless opposition. But by beginning two successive lines with active verbs, Milton sounds completely inspired. However, the *uh* sound in 'nocturnal' starts to dominate, and a tragic note – 'But cloud instead, and ever-during dark/ Surrounds me' – takes over the music of the verse. The *n* in 'expunged' has the effect of lengthening that ugly *uh* sound, but it is sharply shortened by the *t* in 'shut'. This effect is developed in 'much', where in another hoisting movement, Milton moves into the final triumphant passage, which sounds as though it has accomplished what it prays for, as 'I' becomes 'eye'. From 'quite', the *i* sounds become dominant, culminating in 'sight', which rhymes back to 'light' near the start of the first line and at the end of the third. Out of a vast formlessness he has won through.

John Dryden ~ 'To the Memory of Mr Oldham'

Farewell, too little and too lately known,
Whom I began to think and call my own;
For sure our souls were near allied; and thine
Cast in the same poetic mould with mine.
One common note on either lyre did strike,
And knaves and fools we both abhorred alike:
To the same goal did both our studies drive
The last set out the soonest did arrive.
Thus Nisus fell upon the slippery place,
While his young friend performed and won the race.
O early ripe – to thy abundant store
What could advancing age have added more?
It might (what nature never gives the young)
Have taught the numbers of thy native tongue.
But satire needs not those, and wit will shine
Through the harsh cadence of a rugged line:
A noble error, and but seldom made,
When poets are by too much force betrayed.
Thy generous fruits, though gathered ere their prime
Still showed a quickness; and maturing time
But mellows what we write to the dull sweets of rhyme.
Once more, hail and farewell; farewell thou young
But ah too short, Marcellus of our tongue;
Thy brows with ivy, and with laurels bound;
But fate and gloomy night encompass thee around.

John Oldham (1653–83) was twenty-one years Dryden's junior, but he became famous as a satirical poet before Dryden did. Today he is remembered mainly because Dryden wrote this accomplished but anxious elegy for him.

As his classically educated readers would have noticed, Dryden sets up an echo of Catullus' elegy for his brother (No. 91), which ends 'ave atque vale' ('and so hail and farewell'). The grief and loss in the Latin poem is carried into Dryden's by the allusion – the opening line is sad, but beautifully balanced through the repeated *l*s and *t*s, and the *little/lately* consonance and alliteration. The word 'little' here means something like 'we met sporadically and were not close friends', but in an emotional context 'little' – 'wee' in Ireland and Scotland – is an affectionate diminutive, and its *ih* sound is caught once in the next line by 'think', whose *k* sound is repeated by 'call'. This bonds the two monosyllables – all except one word in the line are monosyllables, and this plays against the three bisyllabic words in the first line, which make it slightly faster in pace. The second line is slower, more considered, more intimate, and this sense of closeness – of bonding – is increased by the slightly colloquial 'For sure', which begins the third line and establishes the idea of kinship present in the Catullus allusion. This is the natural freemasonry of poets being brought out into the open – it is as though he is getting to know Oldham after his death.

The enjambment at 'thine' brings even more weight on 'Cast', which begins the line with a strong stress, whereas if the metaphor is both foundry and printing press, with the platen coming down hard and the printer casting off a poem, this poem – with both their names on it – is a joint production. And perhaps both their talents are like pebbles cast in a sling? They know the danger of politics. The next line affirms their joint enterprise – the 'common note'. The lyre develops the classical allusion and gives them personae and distinction, like figures on a Grecian Urn. They are united in contempt for the corrupt and foolish. Both are learned, studious poets in search of fame – classical fame, not mere celebrity – and the younger found it first. Then Dryden cleverly alludes to the moment in Book Five of the *Aeneid* where Nisus in a race slips on the blood of sacrificed oxen, then grabs the front runner's foot to let Euryalus win. Dryden is saying that he helped Oldham gain fame, but he might be saying that by dying Oldham has left the field to him.

Dryden is referring to politics when he uses the word 'slippery' – these are dangerous times for him, as they were for Oldham; indeed Dryden was beaten up by some thugs employed by the poet and courtier Rochester. That phrase 'the harsh cadence of a rugged line' contrasts with this type of slipperiness – cant politics, London street politics – and speaks for a type of defensive anxiety and self-belief in Dryden. He finishes his defence of the Anglican Church, 'Religio Laici', by saying:

> And this unpolished rugged verse I chose,
> As fittest for discourse, and nearest prose,
> For while from sacred truth I do not swerve,
> Tom Sternhold's or Tom Shadwell's rhymes will serve.

He has chosen, he insists, the type of rhymes dull, dogged Whig poets use, and partly this is because he admires a certain rough and ready, blunt, plain-spoken English integrity.

This admiration for a harsh ruggedness is present in 'To My Dear Friend Mr Congreve':

> Well, then, the promised hour is come at last;
> The present Age of wit obscures the past:
> Strong were our Syres and as they Fought they Writ,
> Conqu'ring with force of Arms, and dint of Wit:
> Theirs was the Giant Race, before the Flood;
> And thus, when *Charles* Returned, our Empire Stood.
> Like *Janus* he the stubborn Soil manur'd,
> With rules of Husbandry the rankness cur'd:
> And boisterous *English* Wit, with Art indu'd.
> Our age was cultivated thus at length;
> But what he gained in skill we lost in strength.

That word 'skill' belongs to the 'slippery place', where Nisus fell, while the native rudeness it civilises, but drains force from, resides in the harsh cadences of Oldham's rugged rhymes.

We are also reminded of the episode late in the *Aeneid* where Euryalus' helmet catches the light of the moon during the night attack on the Volsci, betraying their position and causing Nisus to be captured.

Dryden then suggests that Oldham's early ripeness was a type of perfection that could not have been improved on by advancing age. Then in a witty put-down, its inflection signalled by the parenthesis, he suggests that Oldham did not have a very firm grip on English metrics. He then counters this critical judgement with the extenuating remark that satire does not need to be written in perfect metre: 'wit will shine/ Through the harsh cadence of a rugged line.' Here, Dryden's anxiety takes another turn: he is committed to the Augustan enterprise of correct, polished, perfect English. He wants the language to resemble French and to have a polysyllabic nimbleness, grace and delicacy. But he knows that English is a Germanic language, and in his preface to his translation of the *Aeneid*, he speaks of our 'rough, old Teuton monosyllables'. Swift, who disliked the Hanoverian monarchs, who continued the Williamite Revolution, objects to their German names as 'hard, tough, cramp, guttural, harsh, stiff' in his poem 'Directions for a Birthday Song'.

Dryden knows that the English language depends on the struggle between monosyllabic and polysyllabic words. England has emerged from a civil war, Commonwealth and Protectorate into an increasingly shaky restored monarchy. The Whigs, whom Dryden opposed, are agitating to exclude Charles II's brother James, Duke of York, from succeeding to the throne. Charles had no legitimate heir and James was a Catholic, so the future is dangerous and uncertain. When James succeeds in 1685, a year after this poem was written, West Country Dissenters led by the Duke of Monmouth, Charles II's illegitimate son, will rise up in a doomed rebellion against him. For all that Oldham was a professed Tory, his rugged versions of Juvenal link him to all that is robust, bold and liberty-loving in the English language and character. Here, Dryden fears that the success of his own civilising mission has gone too far. His phrase for Oldham's satire – 'too much force' – links him to the Sublime, which is a republican aesthetic.

This is the point of Dryden's highly assured triplet: on the one hand he is demonstrating his mastery of English metrics, on the other he is saying that this degree of skill is a form of pure professional competence, which lacks the quick of life, the force and surprise of genuine risk. The third line of the triplet is a perfect alexandrine: 'But mellows what we write to the dull sweets of rhyme.'

The repeated *ts* in this six-foot line give it a slightly tinny timbre, and there is some anxiety in his use of 'prime', because here he is alluding to another elegy, Milton's 'Lycidas': 'For Lycidas is dead, dead ere his prime'. That supremely great poem is altogether beyond anything that Dryden's perfect couplets could ever encompass. Also we know from his prose that Dryden wanted to write a great epic poem, but, as he remarked after *Paradise Lost* was published in 1667, 'this poet has cut us all out'. He tried to write an epic of King Arthur and his knights but got nowhere, then towards the end of his life he produced a magnificent translation of the *Aeneid*.

He next brings in a translation of Catullus' phrase 'ave atque vale', but he introduces it with another allusion to 'Lycidas', which begins 'Yet once more ye laurels and ye myrtles/ With ivy never sere'. The sense of anxiety and loss deepens at the point, as he echoes Virgil's elegy for Augustus' nephew Marcellus, who was his chosen heir, but who died before Augustus.

The poem ends with an alexandrine, which is like a dead end: Augustus/ Charles/Dryden have failed, they have no heirs. Four years later, William of Orange landed at Torbay and a new Whig regime took over the government of the country. Dryden was stripped of his post as poet laureate and historiographer royal. One of his greatest achievements – the *Aeneid* – lay ahead, a great English poem which is insufficiently studied and celebrated. He is thinking of that poem as he mourns Oldham and contemplates the future.

Alexander Pope ~ 'An Epistle to Miss Blount on her leaving the Town'

As some fond virgin, whom her mother's care
Drags from the town to wholsom country air,
Just when she learns to roll a melting eye,
And hear a spark, yet think no danger nigh;
From the dear man unwilling she must sever,
Yet takes one kiss before she parts for ever:
Thus from the world fair *Zephalinda* flew,
Saw others happy, and with sighs withdrew;
Not that their pleasures caus'd her discontent,
She sigh'd not that They stay'd, but that She went.
She went, to plain-work, and to purling brooks,
Old-fashion'd halls, dull aunts, and croaking rooks,
She went from Op'ra, park, assembly, play,
To morning walks, and pray'rs three hours a day;
To pass her time 'twixt reading and Bohea,
To muse, and spill her solitary Tea,
Or o'er cold coffee trifle with the spoon,
Count the slow clock, and dine exact at noon;
Divert her eyes with pictures in the fire,
Hum half a tune, tell stories to the squire;
Up to her godly garret after sev'n,
There starve and pray, for that's the way to heav'n,
Some Squire, perhaps, you take delight to rack;
Whose game is Whisk, whose treat a toast in sack,
Who visits with a gun, presents you birds,
Then gives a smacking buss, and cries – No words!
Or with his hound comes hollowing from the stable,
Makes love with nods, and knees beneath a table;
Whose laughs are hearty, tho' his jests are coarse,

And loves you best of all things – but his horse.
In some fair evening, on your elbow laid,
You dream of triumphs in the rural shade;
In pensive thought recall the fancy'd scene,
See Coronations rise on ev'ry green;
Before you pass th' imaginary sights
Of Lords, and Earls, and Dukes, and garter'd Knights;
While the spread Fan o'ershades your closing eyes;
Then give one flirt, and all the vision flies.
Thus vanish sceptres, coronets, and balls,
And leave you in lone woods, or empty walls.
So when your slave, at some dear, idle time,
(Not plagu'd with headachs, or the want of rhime)
Stands in the streets, abstracted from the crew,
And while he seems to study, thinks of you:
Just when his fancy points your sprightly eyes,
Or sees the blush of soft *Parthenia* rise,
Gay pats my shoulder, and you vanish quite; .
Streets, chairs, and coxcombs rush upon my sight;
Vext to be still in town, I knit my brow,
Look sow'r, and hum a tune – as you may now.

Poems depend on rhythms, but they also need pauses, sometimes deep pauses, that say more than words or rhythms can, and remind us that silence can state its own meaning. The end and purpose of Pope's brief verse epistle is the pause at the end. This is a love poem that does not quite speak its name.

The first verse paragraph employs the fashionable Latin name assumed by Teresa Blount in a lengthy correspondence with a Mr H. More of Fawley Hall, who wrote under the name Alexis. Her less feisty younger sister, Martha, whom Pope was to become much closer to, and who was rumoured to be his lover, was referred to as

Parthenesia by Lord Chesterfield, and Pope adapts that name towards the end. Martha was also known as Patsy, and was the recipient of Pope's 'Epistle to a Lady', which his biographer, Maynard Mack, says is 'the finest tribute that any eighteenth-century woman ever received'. Pope later liked his readers to think that the earlier, shorter poem was also addressed to Patsy.

Pope has borrowed the opening 'As' from Dryden's prologues and epilogues to his plays, which often begin with an extended simile. The tone is theatrical, witty, artificial, high on adrenalin. The *flew/drew* rhyme, with its long open *oo* sound, designing a type of high-pitched coo, which is quite destroyed by the *went/tent* rhyme that clicks shut like a lock with a reverberating finality on 'went', which sounds absolute, decisive, totally imprisoning. The *w* in 'went' is picked up by 'work' and the spondee 'plāin-wōrk' arrests and imprisons the line. The adjective plus noun formations that follow are typically eighteenth century, deliberate clichés, while 'purling' acknowledges that rivers are said to move in a purling motion, but domestic knitting or purling is also meant, so this is another claustrophobic image. The nouns which follow have no qualifying adjectives – 'Op'ra, park assembly, play' – a phrase which takes the plosives in 'plain' and 'purling' and redefines them as fun, like sparks.

The country, in the eyes of the eighteenth-century wit, is boring, and Pope supplies Hogarthian cartoons of its claustrophobic tedium, the black tea (Bohea) and cold coffee. The internal chime between 'reading' and 'Bohea' insists there is no difference between either. There may be a sexual joke in the spilt tea and the spoon she fiddles with, and another one in her humming half a tune (Pope uses double entendres in other poems and liked to give the impression he was a rake). He obliquely attributes sexual fantasies to her, as she sees pictures in the fire while humming only half a tune, because there is no other half to respond. The grating *k* sounds which began with 'work' are picked up again in 'cold coffee', 'clock', 'exact'. This is the texture of tedium.

Pope's comic portrait of the squire makes the point that unlike that robust philistine he is not intrusive, does not force his attentions on her, and though he has a perfect command of language is not addressing words of endearment directly to her. The *k* sounds reappear in 'rack', 'Whisk' and 'sack'. They culminate in 'smacking buss', a vulgar word which suggests that he's pulled her tight against his chest and planted his wet lips on her cheek. Perhaps Pope is hinting that she would be better receiving kisses and addresses from him? She ought to admit, he implies, that there is a current of desire running under their friendship and epistles. Wittily, he introduces an anticipation of the final pause, when he says that the squire 'loves you best of all things – but his horse'. From 'hound', 'hollowing', 'hearty' to 'horse', the run of *h*s insist on his hearty hollowness.

Taking up the fantasy theme again, he introduces a Spenserian vision in which she is the Faerie Queene or Una waiting for a knight to serve her. He is also making fun of women's liking for romantic novels. The flirting fan again brings in sexual teasing, as Pope carries her loneliness over to his. The 'lone woods, or empty walls' is an imprisoning effect: the walls are bereft of projected fantasies, and both they and the woods carry a dragging adjective, unlike the nouns in the previous lines. It's then that Pope gets personal: he is her 'slave', prone to bad health and writer's block, but like her prone to fantasies – all of which are directed at her 'sprightly', witty, teasing eyes. Notice the way he introduces 'dear', ostensibly to describe the moment when he's not plagued with a headache and writer's block, but really to define a time when he is thinking of her.

It's then that he launches the last tender, inclusive or embracing line: 'Look sow'r, and hum a tune – as you may now'. The chime of 'sow'r' and 'now' bridges the emphatic caesura, which designs the significant pause that reminds them both of her humming half a tune earlier. Here, he adds the other half – or gives the whole tune – and this pairing is reflected both in the complete rhyme and in the way 'now' kisses 'sow'r' and lifts its tetchiness up into the perfect present moment. His knitted brow is a version of the 'plain-work', the purling threads, she must have been doing in the country – they may be separated but they are together in their boredom and pastimes. Out of his 'tune' he draws her 'you', so that the line is intimate, perfectly keyed to the conversational speaking voice.

The same is true of the opening of his verse essay 'On the Characters of Women':

> Nothing so true as what you once let fall,
> 'Most women have no Characters at all.'

It's Mary Wollestonecraft's point about the cultural construction of female or 'feminine' personality in *The Rights of Women*, not a male author ventriloquising a sexist remark – and Pope was feminist in his sympathies with women. The couplet is offhand, lethally observant of society women, with a little pause after 'true', a pause at the end of the line, another after 'women', then an ever so slight pause after 'Characters'. These pauses create and enforce authority, they prevent the couplet from sounding glib and they follow the rhythms of the speaking voice.

We can see this use of the pause in Christina Rossetti's poetry, most wittily in her poem to a would-be lover which ends 'But as for love – no thank you, John.' Pauses have power, they contain and express desire, or they signify rejection, and those energies are crammed into the final pause of Pope's poem, before the kiss in the here-and-now of its final rhyme.

Jonathan Swift ~ 'A Description of a City Shower'

Careful observers may foretell the hour
(By sure prognostics) when to dread a shower.
While rain depends, the pensive cat gives o'er
Her frolics, and pursues her tail no more.
Returning home at night you find the sink
Strike your offended sense with double stink.
If you be wise, then go not far to dine,
You spend in coach-hire more than save in wine.
A coming shower your shooting corns presage,
Old aches throb, your hollow tooth will rage:
Sauntering in coffee-house is Dulman seen;
He damns the climate, and complains of spleen.

Meanwhile the south, rising with dabbled wings,
A sable cloud athwart the welkin flings;
That swilled more liquor than it could contain,
And like a drunkard gives it up again.
Brisk Susan whips her linen from the rope,
While the first drizzling shower is born aslope:
Such is that sprinkling which some careless quean
Flirts on you from her mop, but not so clean:
You fly, invoke the gods; then turning, stop
To rail; she singing, still whirls on her mop.
Nor yet the dust had shunned the unequal strife,
But aided by the wind, fought still for life;
And wafted with its foe by violent gust,
'Twas doubtful which was rain, and which was dust.
Ah! where must needy poet seek for aid,
When dust and rain at once his coat invade?
Sole coat, where dust cemented by the rain
Erects the nap, and leaves a cloudy stain.

Now in contiguous drops the flood comes down,
Threatening with deluge this devoted town.
To shops in crowds the daggled females fly,
Pretend to cheapen goods, but nothing buy.
The templar spruce, while every spout's abroach,
Stays till 'tis fair, yet seems to call a coach.
The tucked-up seamstress walks with hasty strides,
While streams run down her oiled umbrella's sides.
Here various kinds by various fortunes led,
Commence acquaintance underneath a shed.
Triumphant Tories, and desponding Whigs,
Forget their feuds, and join to save their wigs.
Boxed in a chair the beau impatient sits,
While spouts run clattering o'er the roof by fits;
And ever and anon with frightful din
The leather sounds; he trembles from within.
So when Troy chairmen bore the wooden steed,
Pregnant with Greeks, impatient to be freed;
(Those bully Greeks, who, as the moderns do,
Instead of paying chairmen, run them through)
Laocoon struck the outside with his spear,
And each imprisoned hero quaked for fear.

Now from all parts the swelling kennels flow,
And bear their trophies with them as they go:
Filths of all hues and odours, seem to tell
What streets they sailed from, by the sight and smell.
They, as each torrent drives with rapid force
From Smithfield, or St Pulchre's shape their course;
And in huge confluent join at Snow Hill ridge,
Fall from the conduit prone to Holborn Bridge.
Sweepings from butchers' stalls, dung, guts, and blood,
Drowned puppies, stinking sprats, all drenched in mud,
Dead cats and turnip-tops come tumbling down the flood.

Swift was fascinated by coarse, ugly language and the way it challenges polished, polite language. The division between the Yahoos and the Houyhnhnms is one version of this conflict, and so is one of his most successful short poems, 'An Epigram on Scolding':

> Great folks are of a finer mould;
> Lord! How politely they can scold;
> While a coarse English tongue will itch,
> For whore and rogue; and dog and bitch.

His obsession with skin involves a fascination with itchiness – he has a servant girl in Brobdingnag called Glumdalclitch – and he wants his writing often to import an unease and anxiety caused by unpleasant ugly, dissonant words, which as in the epigram clash with everything represented by 'politely'.

He begins his description of the city shower with an eloquent classical confidence. The 'careful Observers' and the noun 'prognostics' lead on naturally to those linked, rather precious words 'depends' (meaning 'impends') and 'pensive'. But 'prognostics' is ugly, its final guttural taking more and rougher stress from the initial guttural in 'Careful'. This sound is picked up by *frolics sink strike sink*, with the result that the *sink/stink* rhyme appears to double *stink*. This is the itchy texture of a rough English tongue, but Swift's ear is also running with a series of sibilant sounds in these lines, which replicate and extend the phrase 'City Shower'. The effect is physical as we can feel in the hard emphasis on 'Strike', which like 'stink' combines both sounds, and which gives that word more emphasis through its initial *st*.

Acutely observant, Swift catches the tense, electrical atmosphere just before the weather breaks – the way the charged atmosphere affects smell is particularly telling. Swift activates the senses in a prickly, uncomfortable manner. The three strong stresses on 'Old aches throb' make that guttural *k* sound part of its pulsing texture.

The line 'A sable cloud athwart the welkin flings' is particularly ugly. The poetic and heraldic word 'sable' echoes 'dabbled' in the previous line, but it belongs to polished discourse, unlike the nautical 'athwart', which backs onto the poetical 'welkin' whose 'in' is caught by the colloquial 'flings'. This is a dissonant, uncomfortable, slightly daft line, which contrives to sound both a bit precious and homemade. The quick motion of the *ih* in 'flings' now spreads through the next five lines, vomiting rain like pigswill.

This sound becomes sharp and decisive in 'Brisk Susan whips her linen from the rope', but the lines then become soggy as the *s* sounds dominate – 'drizzling shower', 'aslope', 'such', 'sprinkling', 'some careless'. Analysing this poem, a student commented on the dryness of its opening line, adding that these later lines are 'a poetic piece of soggy toast'. Swift is designing a damp, formless mulch of words, as a battle is fought between dust and rain. With the mention of 'wind', we get a farting, faecal commotion, which has been prepared for earlier by 'sink'. But this commotion is at the same time a parody of God breathing life into dust to create Adam. The dust here becomes a kind of monster fighting for its life – there is a cartoon-like animism at work here. The battle between opposites, the cementing of dust and rain, is analogous to the linguistic mulch Swift is stirring. The phrase 'Erects the nap' is on one remote level a parody of Adam's creation, with the odd, accurate technicality of 'nap' adding a sudden perkiness. What is created is a cloudy stain like the poem itself.

Swift's observing eye also notes the oiled sides of the seamstress's umbrella. At the same time, he enjoys the social chaos, the mixing up of classes and people with different political opinions, as everyone is thrown together by this emergency. The monosyllabic, Anglo-Saxon 'shed' acts as a buffer to the classical 'Commence acquaintance'. But he immediately returns to the epic, classical world by transforming the sedan chair into the Wooden Horse. This is another mock-epic, like Adam's creation, and it is subsumed by the longer, apocalyptic idea of a cleansing deluge, Noah's Flood swamping a chaotic, selfish, trivial society.

Many of Swift's poems are written in octosyballic couplets – their basic, unvaried, unmusical cadences induce a type of nausea, like travel sickness. Travelling between England and Ireland and its discomforts is one of his subjects:

> Lo here I sit at Holy Head
> With muddy ale and mouldy bread
> All Christian vitals stink of fish
> I'm where my enemyes would wish.

He has a disgusted attraction to monosyllables, which in another poem he calls cramped.

In the line 'The templar spruce, while every spout's abroach', the law student may be spruce, but this line certainly isn't – it is ugly and unkempt. Similarly, rhyming 'Whigs' with 'wigs' is sloppy and lazy – deliberately so, because this is an extended exercise in bad taste. This culminates in the deluge in the closing lines, where St Pulchre's stands out like a swollen boil. The name is short for St Sepulchre's, which brings a tomb into the picture, though paradoxically the abbreviated word suggests the Latin for beautiful, *pulchra*. The *uh* in this word is repeated by 'butcher's stalls, dung, guts, and blood'. And it is carried on in the last two lines, culminating in 'flood'. The closing triplet is a parody of Dryden, with a final grotty alexandrine. Swift was remembering a line in one of Dryden's translations of Virgil's *Georgics*: 'And cakes of Ice came rolling down the Flood'. He was related to Dryden, who, upon reading some of his poems, said, 'Cousin Swift, you are no poet.' Swift is mocking Dryden's habit of occasionally using triplets, which combine two iambic pentameters with an alexandrine, but he is also raging against the idea of the poetic and the beautiful. The world he describes is without form and void, all shapeless bits and pieces, smelly dreck. Swift's classical republican imagination admires the cleansing, restoring effect of the shower.

Samuel Taylor Coleridge ~ 'Frost at Midnight'

The Frost performs its secret ministry,
Unhelped by any wind. The owlet's cry
Came loud – and hark, again! loud as before.
The inmates of my cottage, all at rest,
Have left me to that solitude, which suits
Abstruser musings: save that at my side
My cradled infant slumbers peacefully.
'Tis calm indeed! so calm, that it disturbs
And vexes meditation with its strange
And extreme silentness. Sea, hill, and wood,
This populous village! Sea, and hill, and wood,
With all the numberless goings-on of life,
Inaudible as dreams! the thin blue flame
Lies on my low-burnt fire, and quivers not;
Only that film, which fluttered on the grate,
Still flutters there, the sole unquiet thing.
Methinks, its motion in this hush of nature
Gives it dim sympathies with me who live,
Making it a companionable form,
Whose puny flaps and freaks the idling Spirit
By its own moods interprets, every where
Echo or mirror seeking of itself,
And makes a toy of Thought.

But O! how oft,
How oft, at school, with most believing mind,
Presageful, have I gazed upon the bars,
To watch that fluttering *stranger*! and as oft
With unclosed lids, already had I dreamt
Of my sweet birth-place, and the old church-tower,

Whose bells, the poor man's only music, rang
From morn to evening, all the hot Fair-day,
So sweetly, that they stirred and haunted me
With a wild pleasure, falling on mine ear
Most like articulate sounds of things to come!
So gazed I, till the soothing things, I dreamt,
Lulled me to sleep, and sleep prolonged my dreams!
And so I brooded all the following morn,
Awed by the stern preceptor's face, mine eye
Fixed with mock study on my swimming book:
Save if the door half opened, and I snatched
A hasty glance, and still my heart leaped up,
For still I hoped to see the *stranger's* face,
Townsman, or aunt, or sister more beloved,
My play-mate when we both were clothed alike!

Dear Babe, that sleepest cradled by my side,
Whose gentle breathings, heard in this deep calm,
Fill up the interspersèd vacancies
And momentary pauses of the thought!
My babe so beautiful! it thrills my heart
With tender gladness, thus to look at thee,
And think that thou shalt learn far other lore,
And in far other scenes! For I was reared
In the great city, pent 'mid cloisters dim,
And saw nought lovely but the sky and stars.
But *thou*, my babe! shalt wander like a breeze
By lakes and sandy shores, beneath the crags
Of ancient mountain, and beneath the clouds,
Which image in their bulk both lakes and shores
And mountain crags: so shalt thou see and hear
The lovely shapes and sounds intelligible
Of that eternal language, which thy God
Utters, who from eternity doth teach

Himself in all, and all things in himself.
Great universal Teacher! he shall mould
Thy spirit, and by giving make it ask.

Therefore all seasons shall be sweet to thee,
Whether the summer clothe the general earth
With greenness, or the redbreast sit and sing
Betwixt the tufts of snow on the bare branch
Of mossy apple-tree, while the nigh thatch
Smokes in the sun-thaw; whether the eave-drops fall
Heard only in the trances of the blast
Or if the secret ministry of frost
Shall hang them up in silent icicles,
Quietly shining to the quiet Moon.

This poem was in Keats's mind when he composed 'To Autumn'. He admired Coleridge and once met him on Hampstead Heath. By that time, Coleridge had long abandoned his extreme support for the French Revolution and become a conservative, but Keats, who was friends with Coleridge's former friend, Hazlitt, remained true to a republican position.

Keats would have recognised that 'secret ministry' carries a political charge – 'ministry' in those days meant 'government', not as now a government department. The word 'secret' suggests espionage, and at this time – February 1798 – a government spy was reporting back to Whitehall on Wordsworth and Coleridge. The word 'performs' reinforces this, as it disturbs the windless silence. It's as though a spell is being cast. The *oo* sound in 'solitude' is picked up by the slightly pretentious 'abstruser musings' to subtly bring in the *toowhit-toowhoo* implicit in the mention of the owlet's cry – it emphasises the atmosphere of intense concentration.

This opening line provides the title of a critical study, *Coleridge's*

Secret Ministry, which stresses the occult activism present in this and other poems of this period. The author of the study, Kelvin Everest, observes that the verb 'performs' reinforces the sense of a task that has to be done, 'a task that is at once lonely and isolated, introspective and wary, and yet very important, full of potential and implication, like that of a secret agent'.

Coleridge was writing at a time of widespread social discontent in Britain and Ireland. A bloody revolutionary uprising was to break out in Ireland that summer, and there was a failed French invasion of the country that year. There had been a minor French landing near Fishguard in February 1797.

Coleridge wants to show how the public world of politics can infiltrate the domestic, private world, but he also wants to hold on to an idea of sacred and inviolable privacy. Deep down in his political subconscious, he is becoming disillusioned with radical politics. The French invasion of Switzerland that month contributed to this, and the idea of secrecy partly touches on the buried beginnings of a change of heart that was to lead him to espouse a conservative position.

He introduces anxiety by experimenting with a three-beat phrase, 'Sea, hill, and wood', which he repeats as 'Sea, and hill, and wood'. Both versions seem to reinforce the idea of a perfectly unified landscape linked to the 'populous village'. But then he crams three strong stresses together in 'the thin blue flame', and repeats them in 'sole unquiet'. The little fluttering piece of ash is known in folklore as a 'stranger', and Coleridge uses the term.

The freakish stranger is meant to represent the perils and stresses of being an isolated poet and public intellectual. But he uses this moment to make a bridge to an uncomplicated, childhood happiness: 'sweet birth-place' and 'old church-tower' repeat the three-beat figure and drain it of anxiety. On one level the stranger represents the possibility of a French invasion.

The social awareness in 'the poor man's only music' brings the three beats back, and so does 'hot Fair-day', where there is also a certain discomfort. It may be that the source of the discomfort lies in a buried allusion to a famous moment in *Paradise Lost* where Mulciber – Vulcan – is thrown out of heaven:

> from morn
> To noon he fell, from noon to dewy eve,
> A summer's day; and with the setting sun
> Dropped from the zenith like a falling star.

Coleridge's phrase 'From morn to evening' echoes this passage, which presages the fall of Adam and Eve.

He returns to melodious iambics until 'door half opened' brings anticipation and movement into the musical run of the lines. But he seems to be bringing everything harmoniously together, until the final verse paragraph, which sounds like the conclusion to an argument:

> Therefore all seasons shall be sweet to thee,
> Whether the summer clothe the general earth
> With greenness, or the redbreast sit and sing
> Betwixt the tufts of snow on the bare branch
> Of mossy apple-tree, while the nigh thatch
> Smokes in the sun-thaw; whether the eve-drops fall
> Heard only in the trances of the blast,
> Or if the secret ministry of frost
> Shall hang them up in silent icicles,
> Quietly shining to the quiet Moon.

The lines move nimbly, sweetly, as they build the illusion of a voice that is present as we read. The cradled baby doubles as the reader, so the lines gain in immediacy and warmth. But the robin's red breast – as Keats would have noticed – carries somewhere the idea of blood, of redcoat soldiers. But the real problem begins after the mossy apple-tree, where the two thudding stresses on 'nigh thatch' push down on 'Smōkes' to make it stand out strongly, before the two strong stresses in 'sūn-thāw' pick up the *th* in 'thatch'. As a result, the caesura is stretched too far, the line effectively splits in two as the three-beat figure returns with a vengeance in 'ēve-drōps fāll'. This clutch of stresses comes out of ballad rhythm, out of the poor man's other music, and Coleridge used that rhythm to subtle effect in 'Christabel', where the line 'The thīn grāy cloūd is sprēad on hīgh' contains it. Somewhere the idea of eavesdropping – of spying – is implicit in these closing lines.

Looking at them, I recall that there was great anxiety at this time that the French might invade England, so I see gunsmoke and burning thatch as well as blood. There is a buried, even secret allusion to a speech in *Henry V* where the Constable of France laments the successes of the invading English army:

> And shall our quick blood, spirited with wine,
> Seem frosty? O, for honour of our land,
> Let us not hang like roping icicles
> Upon our houses' thatch, whiles a more frosty people
> Sweat droplets of gallant youth in our rich fields.

In order to try to overcome his fear of a French invasion of England, Coleridge subconsciously alludes to a successful English invasion of France, but the anxiety remains and it weighs on the closing lines. The fact that the secret ministry of frost may 'hang . . . up' the eave-drops in 'silent icicles' gives emphasis to that sinister verb 'hang'. Also the *i* sounds are too numerous, and the repetition of 'quiet' is somehow glib. The last two lines wrap the poem up too neatly after that broken-backed line five lines from the end. By repeating the phrase 'secret ministry' Coleridge shows that he is pleased with it, but by returning us to the first line he makes the poem somehow circular and self-admiring. Keats does not make this mistake in 'To Autumn', an altogether greater poem, but one which is influenced by Coleridge's political pastoral.

Samuel Taylor Coleridge ~ 'Kubla Khan'

In Xanadu did Kubla Khan
A stately pleasure-dome decree:
Where Alph, the sacred river, ran
Through caverns measureless to man
Down to a sunless sea.
So twice five miles of fertile ground
With walls and towers were girdled round:
And there were gardens bright with sinuous rills,
Where blossomed many an incense-bearing tree;
And here were forests ancient as the hills,
Enfolding sunny spots of greenery.

But oh! that deep romantic chasm which slanted
Down the green hill athwart a cedarn cover!
A savage place! as holy and enchanted
As e'er beneath a waning moon was haunted
By woman wailing for her demon-lover!
And from this chasm, with ceaseless turmoil seething,
As if this earth in fast thick pants were breathing,
A mighty fountain momently was forced:
Amid whose swift half-intermitted burst
Huge fragments vaulted like rebounding hail,
Or chaffy grain beneath the thresher's flail:
And 'mid these dancing rocks at once and ever
It flung up momently the sacred river.
Five miles meandering with a mazy motion
Through wood and dale the sacred river ran,
Then reached the caverns measureless to man,
And sank in tumult to a lifeless ocean:

And 'mid this tumult Kubla heard from far
Ancestral voices prophesying war!
The shadow of the dome of pleasure
Floated midway on the waves;
Where was heard the mingled measure
From the fountain and the caves.
It was a miracle of rare device,
A sunny pleasure-dome with caves of ice!

A damsel with a dulcimer
In a vision once I saw:
It was an Abyssinian maid,
And on her dulcimer she played,
Singing of Mount Abora.
Could I revive within me
Her symphony and song,
To such a deep delight 'twould win me,
That with music loud and long,
I would build that dome in air,
That sunny dome! those caves of ice!
And all who heard should see them there,
And all should cry, Beware! Beware!
His flashing eyes, his floating hair!
Weave a circle round him thrice,
And close your eyes with holy dread,
For he on honey-dew hath fed,
And drunk the milk of Paradise.

The story of this poem's composition is legendary: if a person from the neighbouring village of Porlock hadn't knocked at Coleridge's door, he would have finished writing out the poem of two to three hundred lines he had composed in his sleep. Coleridge had fallen asleep over a travel book called *Purchas his Pilgrimage* by William Purchas, which was published in 1617. This story of the poem's composition inspired a famous critical study, *The Road to Xanadu* by John Livingston Lowes, which was published in 1927 and is held in great reverence by literary scholars who cannot now write in the manner of Lowes:

> We set out long ago, through a glimmering chaos across which lingered, faintly luminous, like the tracks of shining creatures in the sea, the trace of the adventuring imagination. And by strange and devious ways that glimmering track has led us into the trodden highway of the creative energy.

Lowes shows how Coleridge's vast reading – 'I have read almost everything,' he said – shapes this mysterious poem.

It begins as an orientalist fantasy, but the internal rhyme 'Xan' and 'Khan' boxes in the subject. The first consonant of 'Xan' is pronounced like a z, so when we reach 'Alph', it's as is we've gone backwards through the alphabet, implied by 'Alph', from *z* to *a*. This could be called a reactionary movement, and it was a track Coleridge was shortly to take. Coleridge the young Jacobin is thinking about the state, which is touched on in the word 'stately'. He is thinking about the relationship between art and power, so that the pleasure garden, reminiscent of the Garden of Eden, appears to be planted on top of Minotaur's Labyrinth, a system of subterranean jails. The gardens are beautiful but that word 'sinuous', used once by Milton in *Paradise Lost*, brings danger into the ordered paradisal image. Milton describes how on the sixth day of creation insects and worms teemed out of the earth, 'Streaking the ground with sinuous traces'. This is before the Fall, but those 'sinuous traces' are what Milton four lines later calls 'snaky folds'. Coleridge's phrase releases itself suddenly because the movement of the line is arrested by the monosyllabic 'bright', which catches the force of the four *i* sounds in the sixth line. Then, in order to allow the easy anapaestic movement of *uous rills* to complete itself, the iambic foot 'with sin' draws a pun out of the adjective and makes a noun which is mentioned forty-five times in *Paradise Lost*. Milton uses 'incense' in the poem to mean the precious perfume – incense, myrrh and gold – but he also uses it as a verb, 'incensed', to mean angry. These might be trees whose perfumed blossoms could turn into dangerous fruit.

What drives the opening lines is the pattern of repeated *d* sounds which culminate in 'demon-lover' (line 16). The long *ee* sounds in 'demon' pick up 'Deep' in line twelve, which passes it on to 'green' and 'cedarn' in the next. The paradox is that these gardens contain forests – the gardens are huge, but as they're girdled round with walls and towers, we would not expect them to hold wilderness, forest. These deep green places with their 'sunny spots' – glades – speak to the English love of the Greenwood, to a love of freedom which challenges what was called the Norman Yoke. In this poem Coleridge invents the word 'greenery'.

It's here that the poem appears to put under pressure the order it has designed following Kubla Khan's fiat. This is a sublime moment as the 'deep romantic chasm' appears to break the poem open by introducing that republican aesthetic, the sublime (the beautiful belongs to monarchical courtly culture). The guttural *k*s, the exclamation marks, the words 'savage' and 'demon' introduce a historical anxiety into the poem.

From the first line, Coleridge's ear is running with *d* sounds, perhaps because he is subconsciously concerned by despotism. This poem appears to celebrate the autonomous work of art, but its orientalist and primitivist surface is disturbed by a sudden violent eruption:

> A mighty fountain momently was forced:
> Amid whose swift half-intermitted burst
> Huge fragments vaulted like rebounding hail,
> Or chaffy grain beneath the thresher's flail:
> And mid these dancing rocks at once and ever
> It flung up momently the sacred river.

Kubla Kahn re-established the unity of the Chinese state, and an idea of the state is imaged in the labyrinthine river, which runs 'through caverns measureless to man'. The river erupts in an image which refers to revolutionary violence – a violence that is given emphatically temporal movement through the repeated adverb 'momently', which means both 'in a moment' and 'of moment', i.e. important. Coleridge wants to express the moment-by-moment movement – the content – of present political action, but he also wants to soften and distance such action historically and geographically. As a result, readings of this poem tend to stress its exoticism and the myth of its incompletion, rather than considering its situation in a decade of revolutionary struggle. But the ancestral voices that prophesy war in 'Kubla Khan' issue from the struggles of European nations. It is their violence and their responsibility for war and empire which Coleridge seeks to offload on to this 'romantic chasm', this 'savage place'.

An exception to the ahistorical readings of Coleridge is a study by Carl Woodring, *Politics in the Poetry of Coleridge*, where he argues that the poem exults in the disruption of the sacred river. Coleridge associated caves of ice with Russian despotism – he had a particular hatred for Catherine the Great, whose predecessor, Empress Anna, had decreed, 'in a despotic whim', the construction of an ice palace. This was condemned by Cowper in *The Task*:

> Silently as a dream the fabric rose;
> No sound of hammer or of saw was there.
> Ice upon ice, the well-adjusted parts
> Were soon conjoin'd, nor other cement ask'd
> Than water interfused to make them one.
> Lamps gracefully disposed, and of all hues,
> Illumined every side; a watery light
> Gleam'd through the clear transparency, that seem'd
> Another moon new risen, or meteor fallen
> From heaven to earth, of lambent flame serene.

> So stood the brittle prodigy, though smooth
> And slippery the materials, yet frostbound
> Firm as a rock. Nor wanted aught within,
> That royal residence might well befit,
> For grandeur or for use. Long wavy wreaths
> Of flowers, that fear'd no enemy but warmth,
> Blush'd on the panels.

A note explains that the Empress Anna constructed a palace of ice on the bank of the Neva, which lasted from January to March 1740. Cowper then criticises the 'great playthings' of powerful princes, and his unrelenting radical morality must have touched Coleridge, who at this period was published by the left-wing Joseph Johnson, who also published Cowper. Anna ruled from 1730 to 1740 through a clique of German advisers, who employed excessively brutal means of suppressing opposition.

Coleridge had used the image of what he called 'the Russian palace of ice, glittering, cold and transitory', some years before, as a pejorative. History, we can see, has infiltrated Coleridge's imagination, and two years later he wrote a piece of journalism for the *Morning Post* in which he compared the deceitful language of the prime minister, William Pitt, to a palace. The Whig parliamentarian Charles James Fox had approached that palace like 'some good genius', and at 'the first touch of his word' that 'spell-built palace of the state magician' had tumbled down on the head of 'the wizard that had reared it'.

Pitt, if anyone, was the man of the moment as he led Britain against revolutionary France – that word 'momently' carries many significances as I've suggested, among them weight, importance and transitoriness. It catches the now of political action, while the 'chaffy grain' could be the newspaper commentaries on the heavy fragments flying from the explosions. The word 'momently' has the effect of emphasising 'mazy motion', 'measureless to man' and 'tumult' – the *ms* touch each other, and are there again in 'midway', 'mingled measure' and 'miracle'. Interestingly, Coleridge has remembered the phrase 'mingled measure' from Collins's 'The Passions: An Ode for Music':

> Thro' glades and Glooms the mingled Measure stole,
> Or o'er some haunted stream with fond Delay,
> Round an holy Calm diffusing,
> Love of Peace, and lonely Musing,
> In hollow Murmurs died away.

The caverns, we remember, are measureless to man, and so the way music and the measurement of distance are combined links art with politics, because the idea of the labyrinth, of buried prison cells, is present here.

The effect of the echoing *ms*, I think, is to heighten 'dome', which leads on to 'damsel with a dulcimer'. They finally culminate in 'milk', which is redemptive like the milk of human kindness in *Macbeth*. I suspect at some level Coleridge is dramatising the typical oxymoron in Petrarchan love poetry – 'I freeze in fire, I burn in ice' – because fire is present in the flashing eyes of the John the Baptist figure he imagines becoming at the end. So this is also a poem about being in love.

John the Baptist was a rebel and visionary who was decapitated. Five years later Coleridge would become obsessed with the Irish rebel leader, Robert Emmet, who was hanged and then decapitated after leading a failed rebellion in Dublin. Coleridge's friend Southey wrote a poem to Emmet, and one can imagine that the two young English republicans saw Emmet as a romantic hero. At some level 'dome' suggests 'doom', and Coleridge is peering into the historical abyss in this poem, which is an incantatory report from that savage place, but we can lose ourselves in the incantation and be almost free of history.

William Wordsworth ~ from *The Prelude*

Ye lowly cottages in which we dwelt,
A ministration of your own was yours,
A sanctity, a safeguard, and a love.
Can I forget you, being as ye were
So beautiful among the pleasant fields
In which ye stood? Or can I here forget
The plain and seemly countenance with which
Ye dealt out your plain comforts? Yet had ye
Delights and exultations of your own:
Eager and never weary we pursued
Our home amusements by the warm peat fire
At evening, when with pencil and with slate,
In square divisions parcelled out, and all
With crosses and with cyphers scribbled o'er,
We schemed and puzzled, head opposed to head,
In strife too humble to be named in verse;
Or round the naked table, snow-white deal,
Cherry, or maple, sate in close array,
And to the combat – lu or whist – led on
A thick-ribbed army, not as in the world
Neglected and ungratefully thrown by
Even for the very service they had wrought,
But husbanded through many a long campaign.
Uncouth assemblage was it, where no few
Had changed their functions – some, plebean cards
Which fate beyond the promise of their birth
Had glorified, and called to represent
The persons of departed potentates.
Oh, with what echoes on the board they fell!

Ironic diamonds – clubs, hearts, diamonds, spades,
A congregation piteously akin.
Cheap matter did they give to boyish wit,
Those sooty knaves, precipitated down
With scoffs and taunts like Vulcan out of heaven;
The paramount ace, a moon in her eclipse;
Queens, gleaming through their splendour's last decay;
And monarchs, surly at the wrongs sustained
By royal visages. Meanwhile abroad
The heavy rain was falling, or the frost
Raged bitterly with keen and silent tooth;
And, interrupting the impassioned game,
From Esthwaite's neighbouring lake the splitting ice,
While it sank down towards the water, sent
Among the meadows and the hills its long
And dismal yellings, like the noise of wolves
When they are howling round the Bothnic main.

[Book 1, ll 498–542 (1805)]

In his epic, this is one of the most powerful 'spots of time', as Wordsworth called them – moments of intense vision that have stayed with him throughout his life. It begins as the equivalent of a naive painting, which gives grace and dignity to the common people. He gives 'lowly' authority and dignity by repeating the *o* sound in 'own', 'So' and 'home'. This has the effect of emphasising the presence of cottages in the landscape, with a reverberant hum coming out of the repeated *n* sounds, as 'in' is picked up by the polysyllabic 'ministration' in a curious line, which has a rather tautological effect, before the quality being ministered is explained in three emphatic nouns and in the spondee 'safeguard', firmly in the middle of the line.

The phrase 'pleasant fields' is reminiscent of 'Elysian fields', and this has the effect of pushing the cottages back in time, which may be why the cottages are then described as 'plain', which is repeated in the next line. By addressing the cottages as 'ye', he both humanises them and invokes them as gods.

He then moves into the epic recall of the childhood card game, where the long *ee* sounds space out the slow movement of the rapt, thoughtful playing of the game. The adjective 'home' is strengthened by the earlier *o* sounds, so that it stands out and slows the movement of the line for a moment, and then takes warmth, as well as the reverberant *m*, from the warm peat fire. They are doing noughts and crosses, an innocent pastime, except this is an allusion to Milton's republican epic:

> And calculate the stars, how they will wield
> The mighty frame, how build, unbuild, contrive
> To save appearances, how gird the sphere
> With centric and eccentric scribbled o'er.

Wordsworth knows that the metric system was devised during the French Revolution, when France was divided into geometric *départements*, and this makes the noughts and crosses less than innocent. But they also remind him of the passage where Raphael tells Adam that God will laugh at the 'quaint opinions wide' of future men trying to calculate the structure of the universe in eccentric scribbles. The verb 'schemed', with its associations with political manipulation, makes this point. It's as though they're locked, head to head, in political argument. This is struggle, 'strife', but Wordsworth now turns to the lowly and naive, which is too 'humble' to be named in verse.

When he tells us the table is made of 'snow-white deal', we recognise its innocence, and perhaps recognise that the cards are about to be dealt – it is pure and clean, they are dirty and used. But 'naked' is surprising (there is a 'naked pool' late in *The Prelude*), for this is a republican adjective which harks back to Adam and Eve's naked innocence in *Paradise Lost.* But now we are not sure about what word is right for this table – it is deal, cherry, maple, and the vagueness, paradoxically, strengthens the presence of the table. The verb 'slate' picking up 'naked' sounds slightly archaic, and has a military tang to it, a reminiscence of siege warfare where an army sits in front of a town or city.

The cards, which in the innocence of mock epic echo the cards in *The Rape of the Lock*, are 'thick-ribbed,' and this makes them sound like soldiers. Cromwell said he chose 'the free way not the formal', and by this he meant that he chose his officers not according to wealth and background, but according to their ability as soldiers. So with these playing cards, some of whom have been promoted into the aristocracy. But they are described as an 'uncouth assemblage' – a phrase which echoes the six uses of 'uncouth' in *Paradise Lost*, where, for example, Satan finds his 'uncouth way' through hell (2.407). Some lines before this, a murmur has filled the 'assembly' in hell, so in Wordsworth's echo of Milton we also glimpse the French Revolution through the allusion to the English Revolution.

The falling cards echo a famous moment in *Paradise Lost* where the fallen angels are imagined like this: 'Thick as autumnal leaves that strew a vale in Valombrossa'. This is also picked up in 'thick-ribbed', and is followed by an echo of another moment from Milton, where Vulcan, thrown out of heaven, picks up Hephaestus' descent in the *Iliad* and its unforgettable version in *Paradise Lost*:

> From morn
> To noon he fell, from noon to dewy eve,
> A summer's day: and with the setting sun
> Dropped from the zenith like a falling star.

This is a rejection of Royalism, and so is the next image of the eclipsed moon/queen in her 'splendour's last decay'.

There must be a critical echo of Burke's famous tribute to Marie-Antoinette in *Reflections on the Revolution in France*:

> And surely never lighted on this orb, which she hardly seemed to touch, a more delightful vision, I saw her just above the horizon, decorating and cheering the elevated sphere she just began to move in, – glittering like the morning star, full of life, and splendour, and joy.

Wordsworth's epic has to echo Satan's descent in order to affirm its ambitions – ambitions which are unimpressed by the wrongs sustained by 'royal visages'. The heap of greasy slapped-down cards, victors and losers, uncouth new members of the ruling class, is an image of French revolutionary politics, where the card-players are like the Fates or Greek gods deciding the outcome of the intensely concentrated game. They are innocent, inside the moment, but history and hindsight carry fear and terror into the imaginative framing of the episode. The English Revolution – Milton's epic subject – is inside the language and the imagery, too. That 'thick-ribbed army' also suggests a ship, emblem of the state – this is the new republic successfully resisting the armies of the *anciens régimes* of Europe sent to destroy it.

He then shifts to a European vision by a clever pun on 'abroad', which on one level means 'outside the door' and on the other means 'in foreign lands, France, for example'. The splitting ice is another image of the revolutionary crowd, which is brought out more clearly Wordsworth's rewriting of the lines in the 1850 version of *The Prelude*:

> And, attempting oft that eager game,
> For under Esthwaite's splitting fields of ice
> The pent-up air, struggling to free itself,
> Gave out to meadow grounds and hills a loud
> Protracted yelling, like the noise of wolves
> Howling in troops along the Bothnic Main.

The repressed people struggle to free themselves, terrible atrocities take place, and the passage ends in Northern Europe, as wolves howl by the Baltic. It's almost as though Wordsworth is anticipating Napoleon's Russian campaign, as he remembers the wars between Russia and Sweden. The outside world, cold and dangerous, has entered the cosy domestic world, as, like any Marxist, Wordsworth subdues the private to the public. Those howling wolves represent the September Massacres, which took place during his visit to Paris in 1792. But they also echo Milton, who in the last book of *Paradise Lost* achieves this prophecy of religion under the Restoration:

> Wolves shall succeed for teachers, grievous wolves,
> Who all the sacred mysteries of heaven
> To their own, vile advantages shall turn.

The wolves are closer to home, and the older Wordsworth will reach an accommodation with them.

John Keats ~ 'To Autumn'

1

Season of mists and mellow fruitfulness,
Close bosom-friend of the maturing sun,
Conspiring with him how to load and bless
With fruit the vines that round the thatch-eves run;
To bend with apples the moss'd cottage-trees,
And fill all fruit with ripeness to the core;
To swell the gourd, and plump the hazel shells
With a sweet kernel; to set budding more,
And still more, later flowers for the bees,
Until they think warm days will never cease,
For Summer has o'er-brimm'd their clammy cells.

2

Who hath not seen thee oft amid thy store?
Sometimes whoever seeks abroad may find
Thee sitting careless on a granary floor,
Thy hair soft-lifted by the winnowing wind;
Or on a half-reap'd furrow sound asleep,
Drows'd with the fume of poppies while thy hook
Spares the next swath and all its twined flowers:
And sometimes like a gleaner thou dost keep
Steady thy laden head across a brook;
Or by a cyder-press, with patient look,
Thou watchest the last oozings hours by hours.

3

Where are the songs of Spring? Ay, where are they?
Think not of them, thou hast thy music too, –
While barred clouds bloom the soft-dying day,

And touch the stubble-plains with rosy hue;
Then in a wailful choir the small gnats mourn
Among the river sallows, borne aloft
Or sinking as the light wind lives or dies;
And full-grown lambs loud bleat from hilly bourn;
Hedge-crickets sing; and now with treble soft
The red-breast whistles from a garden-croft;
And gathering swallows twitter in the skies.

Opening a school anthology, I find this note to Keats's ode:

> The magnificent ode is justly famous, and is often regarded as the most perfect of Keats's poems. Its structure is quite complex, but after a couple of readings it will not be difficult to see that the first verse describes the 'positive' side of autumn – the side that looks back to summer and brings it to fruition, while the third verse describes the 'negative' side – a suggestion of chilliness, a series of thin sounds, and the sadness of approaching winter. The middle verse balances these two with four glimpses of a figure representing both the spirit of autumn and a farm-worker engaged in a series of typical autumnal activities.

This describes, clearly and sensitively, how the poem has been read since Keats's published it in 1820, but in recent years a group of historical critics has offered a more complicated, political reading of Keats. He was passionately interested in politics, and it would be surprising if that interest didn't shape his writing. As a radical, who read and contributed to John and Leigh Hunt's famous weekly journal, *The Examiner*, he sees not so much a 'farm-worker' as a member of the rural poor, a gleaner, who has scraped up the grains of corn left after the farm labourers had gathered in the harvest. Gleaning was made illegal in 1818, as Keats knew from articles published in *The Examiner*, so by personifying autumn as a gleaner he is characterising the season as a proud and dignified – a 'steady' and we assume tall and stately – young woman.

Keats travelled from London to Winchester on 15 September 1819. Six days later he wrote to his friend Reynolds:

> How beautiful the season is now – How fine the air. A temperate sharpness about it. Really, without joking, chaste weather – Dian skies – I never like'd stubble fields so much as now – Aye better than the chilly green of the spring. Somehow a stubble plain looks warm – in the same way that certain pictures look warm – this struck me so much in my Sunday's walk that I composed upon it.

And so Keats composed his famous ode after a walk beside some stubble fields, and sent it to his friend Richard Woodhouse in a letter he wrote on 21 September 1819.

At this point in his short life, Keats was thinking of becoming a journalist, and he would shortly go to see his friend Hazlitt for advice about this. He followed the political situation closely, predicting in a letter to his brother George that the country was about to erupt, and travelling to London to take part in a mass demonstration, which welcomed 'Orator' Hunt after the Peterloo Massacre on 16 August 1819. In an excited, outraged letter to George, he said it 'would take me a whole day and a quire of paper to give you anything like the detail'. Then in a long letter from Winchester, he gave his brother a homily on liberty and progress, arguing that there should be a continual change 'for the better' in all civilised countries. He says that three great changes have been in progress – 'First for the better, Next for the worse, and a third time for the better once more.' This movement is picked up in the spring passage in the ode, and it leads into this statement:

> The first was the gradual annihilation of the tyranny of the nobles, when Kings found it in their interest to conciliate the common people, elevate them and be just to them. Just when baronial Power ceased and before standing armies were so dangerous, Taxes were few, Kings were lifted by the people over the heads of their nobles, and those people held a rod over Kings. The change for the worse in Europe was again this. The obligation of Kings to the Multitude began to be forgotten. Custom had made noblemen the humble servants of Kings. Then

> Kings turned to the Nobles as adorners of their power, the slaves of it, and from the people as creatures continually endeavouring to check them. Then in every Kingdom there was a long struggle of Kings to destroy all popular privileges. The English were the only people in Europe who made a grand kick at this. They were slaves to Henry 8th but were freemen under William 3rd at the time the French were abject slaves under Lewis 14th. The example of England, and the liberal writers of France and England sowed the seed of opposition to this Tyranny – and it was swelling in the ground till it burst out in the French revolution.

We need to bring this account of the historical process into our reading of the ode: the 'seed of opposition . . . swelling in the ground' is caught up in 'swell the gourd, and plump the hazel shells', where one notices also the adjacency of 'ground' and 'gourd'.

It is history as much as nature which conspires to 'swell the gourd'. Keats's metaphor becomes literal here, but the metaphor survives. Keats divides history into three movements and his poem has three stanzas. The movement from autumn to spring and back to autumn is also tripartite, for it is a different, colder autumn we end with – the robin makes that point. Keats has made his poem flourish by planting 'the seed of opposition'.

If we look closely we can see that this is a pastoral poem which aims to communicate a subtle anxiety and discomfort behind or within its apparently attractive images. The susurruses in the first line begin this, and the word 'mists' takes us back to Milton, whom Keats read very closely: Milton speaks of the 'mists and intricacies of state', and characterises Satan as a mist. The word 'conspiring' alludes to what the Tory press called the 'Manchester conspiracy' – the meeting on St Peter's Fields, where the massacre took place. The *sun run* combination brings *gun* almost to mind, and those loaded apple trees make me uneasy: once apples touch the ground they're prey to slugs and go rotten. The word 'bend' belongs to the language of power, and that phrase 'ripeness to the core' is strange and unsettling – we talk about fruit being rotten to the core, never ripe. There is a similar effect in 'clammy cells', almost a prison image, or a far-off echo of a Manchester sweat shop.

Keats feared for his health – he had a medical training and had just nursed his tubercular brother, Tom, on his deathbed. Those 'clammy cells' speak for that anxiety – and inside 'fill', 'still' and 'will' lurks *ill*. The over-brimming image is a crowd image: Keats had recently been part of a London crowd of 300,000 demonstrating against the tyranny of the government.

Then the poem moves into a slightly listless, drowsy, arrested stanza. Inside its stasis is the idea of winning – 'winnowing wind' has 'win' twice, and this reflects Keats's letter on historical progress. Also 'win' is separate from the rest of the word by the stress it takes, because it picks up the *ih* in 'lifted', effectively making the last foot an anapaest – 'owing wind'. And we obviously get 'win' repeated here – this is the idea of historical victory. That soft-lifted hair is slightly too attractive (the *care/hair* internal rhyme draws attention to this), but this is also an image of a patient being nursed. The poppies hold associations for Keats, as we can see in a letter he wrote to his brother, three years earlier:

> The stalks and blades
> Chequer my tablet with their quivering shades,
> On one side is a field of drooping oats
> Through which the poppies show their scarlet coats,
> So pert and useless that they bring to mind
> The scarlet coats that pester human-kind.

Keats loathed the British Army, and associated its redcoats with poppy blossom. The 'hook' in the ode is both the grim reaper's sickle and a cavalryman's sword, which, in a reprieving action, spares the next swathe. The 'fume of poppies' suggests both an opiate and the reek of gunpowder, because this is also a battlefield, stained red with blood. The following winter, he would cough up blood and say to a friend : 'I know the colour of that blood; – it is arterial blood; – I cannot be deceived in that colour; – that drop of blood is my death-warrant; I must die.'

When gleaning was made illegal, there were articles protesting this in *The Examiner*, to which Keats had contributed poems, some of which expressed republican views. The gleaner is like a scavenger on a battle field, and that *steady/head* internal rhyme puts a trace of *lead* into 'laden', which is another image like 'bend' that belongs to the discourse of power. The adjective 'patient' brings the noun to mind, and the implicitly crushed apples in the cider press make this another crowd image – 'a press' is a term for crowd, and a press gang is a small armed body. The cider press, like the granary floor, is a place of torture, and it is also an echo of this passage in the Book of Revelation (14:19–20):

> And the angel thrust in his sickle into the earth, and gathered the vine of the earth, and cast it into the great winepress of the wrath of God.
> And the winepress was trodden without the city, and blood came out of the winepress, even unto the horse bridles, by the space of a thousand and six hundred furlongs.

The sickle ('hook'), the implicit blood, the ripening fruit are all here, and so is the trodden Peterloo crowd.

That in some ways uncomfortable noun 'oozings' draws out the previous *oo* sounds, and is another deliberate bad-taste moment. This prepares us for the image of a mackerel sky at sunset, where the static 'barred clouds' bring to mind a prison cell, another possibly clammy image of constriction and claustrophobia. The bloom of the soft-dying day is ominous and sinister, partly because the double *d*s back up against it to hint 'doom'. It reminds me of the unreally healthy complexions which patients who are about to die can have (Louis MacNeice's sister, who was a doctor, knew her brother was within days of death from viral pneumonia when she visited him in hospital and noticed how unusually healthy his cheeks looked). The phrase 'soft-dying' takes us back to 'soft-lifted' and to the lingering *care hair Spares* assonance. The word 'bloom' takes an almost explosive amount of stress in the line, as it follows the stressed noun 'clouds'. There are six stresses in the line because 'soft' is also stressed so that 'soft-dy' is a spondee, which arrests the forward movement of a line that doesn't want to end.

The *uh* in 'touch' transferred to 'stubble' is tactile, and we remember Keats's remark about now liking the warm look of such fields. But he would know that stubble continues to grow on the chins of corpses, and would have wanted the 'stub' in that word to suggest *stop*, as well as *stump*, an amputated limb. The 'rosy hue' is again sinister because it is another blood image, which makes the plain resemble a battlefield, where the oddly described 'small gnats' fulfil the purpose of a chorus in a classical elegy – except these are proletarian mourners, hence the adjective 'small'. But, looking at the work of the Keats scholar Noah Comet, I realise that the gnats are also drawn from the *Faerie Queene*, where Sir Guyon and his knights face an army of a thousand 'villeins' who swarm

> Out of the rockes and caues adioyning nye,
> Vile caytiue wretches, ragged, rude, deformd,
> All threatening death, all in straunge manner armd,
> Some with vnweldy clubs, some with long speares.

As the knights hew and slash them, they fade into shadows: 'As when a swarme of gnats at euentide/ Out of the fennes of Allan do arise.' Spenser believed the English should have practised genocide in Ireland, and his lines repeat that belief. Keats, who read his poetry, would not have shared his beliefs, and applies the image implicitly to the actions of the 15th Hussars, the Cheshire Yeomanry Cavalry and the Royal Horse Artillery at St Peter's Fields, as they charged a crowd, many of whom were patriotic veterans of Waterloo who had led the protesters to the fields in military formation.

But there is another allusion in 'small gnats' to Imogen's speech early in *Cymbeline* where she describes Posthumus leaving the shores of Britain. Keats's friend Charles Cowden Clarke never forgot how touched Keats was by this passage, saying:

> Once, when reading the 'Cymbeline' aloud, I saw his eyes fill with tears, and his voiced faltered when he came to the departure of Posthumus, and Imogen saying she would have watched him –
>
> 'Till the diminution
> Of space had pointed him sharp as my needle;
> Nay, followed him till he had *melted from*
> *The smallness of a gnat to air*; and then
> Have turn'd mine eye and wept. (I.iii.18–22)

Keats is remembering this passage in that odd phrase 'small gnats', and locating its grief on St Peter's Fields.

When Keats wrote 'choir' he mis-spelt it as 'quire', a word, we remember, he used in his letter to his brother describing the post-Peterloo demonstration in London. The word brings writing into the image – writing as a witness. The *s*s in 'small gnats' pick up the susurrus in the previous line, and we remember 'oozings hours by hours' and the first line's run of *s* sounds. They are not crisp and clean, those sounds; they're too much like body fluids.

They appear again in 'sallows,' a word which Keats was fond of – it's dialect for 'willows' – but a sallow complexion is not attractive, so this is another uncomfortable word. Willows – weeping willows – are often used on mourning cards, so this is another death image. The word 'born' is echoed in 'bourn', so that I wonder if this is Hamlet's 'bourne from which no traveller returns', and find another image of death here. Soon the ominously full-grown lambs will cross that barrier, as surely as the gleaner with her heavy head has crossed the brook. There are seven packed stresses in this line, and inside that cold verb 'bleat' I see *eat*. The robin may appear slightly sentimental, but Keats didn't think of it like that, remarking in a verse letter to John Hamilton Reynolds, to whom, as he tells his friend Woodhouse, he was going to send 'To Autumn':

> Still do I that most fierce destruction see,
> The shark at savage prey – the hawk at pounce,
> The gentle robin, like a pard or ounce,
> Ravening a worm.

The robin's red breast reflects the poppies, which in turn reflect redcoat soldiers.

The hedge-cricket I take to be a figure for members of the radical underground, preparing to winter out in readiness for the spring. After all, this is how Burke saw them in *Reflections on the Revolution in France*, where the 'importunate chink' of the grasshoppers speaks for the cries of English radicals protesting against the government. There are a lot of *ih* sounds in those lines – *river sinking wind lives hilly crickets sing whistles gathering twitter* – and they are deliberately unattractive, unsettling. Although they gather to a head in 'twitters', the last line, with its image of emigration – to America, like Keats's brother – also brings together what I take to be the three dominant sounds in the poem. These are the gutteral *k*, the sibilant *s*, and the vowel sound *i* .They first come together in 'Conspiring', and they are last packed together in 'skies'. So the end of the poem reprises the beginning, rather as 'swallows' picks up 'sallows'. This is also the last of the liminal, crossing-a-threshold images, and it may have its source in the *Aeneid*, where dead Trojan soldiers are transformed to birds.

Keats's poem alludes to many poems, as scholars such as Noah Comet have wonderfully shown. It may seem controversial to suggest that beyond being a highly and subtly allusive writer, he was also capable of writing coded political poems. But Jane Austen, like Burke, did the same thing, remarking in *Emma* on the landscape around Highbury being a 'sweet view' of 'English verdure, English comfort, seen under a sun bright without being oppressive'. The heat of the sun in the second stanza of Keats's great ode is, I think, meant to be on the verge of being oppressive.

John Clare ~ 'To the Snipe'

Lover of swamps
The quagmire overgrown
With hassock tufts of sedge – where fear encamps
Around thy home alone

The trembling grass
Qμakes from the human foot
Nor bears the weight of man to let him pass
Where he alone and mute

Sitteth at rest
In safety neath the clump
Of hugh flag-forrest that thy haunts invest
Or some old sallow stump

Thriving on seams
That tiney islands swell
Just hilling from the mud and rancid streams
Suiting thy nature well

For here thy bill
Suited by wisdom good
Of rude unseemly length doth delve and drill
The gelid mass for food

And here may hap
When summer suns hath drest
The moors rude desolate and spungy lap
May hide thy mystic nest

Mystic indeed
For isles that ocean make
Are scarcely more secure for birds to build
Then this flag-hidden lake

Boys thread the woods
To their remotest shades
But in these marshy flats these stagnant floods
Security pervades

From year to year
Places untrodden lye
Where man nor boy nor stock hath ventured near
– Nought gazed on but the sky

And fowl that dread
The very breath of man
Hiding in spots that never knew his tread
A wild and timid clan

Wigeon and teal
And wild duck – restless lot
That from mans dreaded sight will ever steal
To the most dreary spot

Here tempests howl
Around each flaggy plot
Where they who dread mans sight the water fowl
Hide and are frighted not

Tis power divine
That heartens them to brave
The roughest tempest and at ease recline
On marshes or the wave

Yet instinct knows
Not safetys bounds to shun
The firmer ground where skulking fowler goes
With searching dogs and gun

By tepid springs
Scarcely one stride across

Though brambles from its edge a shelter flings
Thy safety is at loss

And never chuse
The little sinky foss
Streaking the moores whence spa-red water spews
From puddles fringed with moss

Free booters there
Intent to kill and slay
Startle with cracking guns the trepid air
And dogs thy haunts betray

From dangers reach
Here thou art safe to roam
Far as these washy flag-worn marshes stretch
A still and quiet home

In these thy haunts
Ive gleaned habitual love
From the vague world where pride and folly taunts
I muse and look above

Thy solitudes
The unbounded heaven esteems
And here my heart warms into higher moods
And dignifying dreams

I see the sky
Smile on the meanest spot
Giving to all that creep or walk or flye
A calm and cordial lot

Thine teaches me
Right feelings to employ
That in the dreariest places peace will be
A dweller and a joy

This is one of the greatest nature poems in the language. Clare wrote it in 1817, and though it has been reprinted fairly often it has yet to be properly recognised as the masterpiece it is.

It begins on Whittlesey Mere, a watery wilderness before it was drained and cultivated. But in the description of the 'hassock tufts' of sedge in the third line, Clare immediately brings a country churchyard to mind (hassocks are small upholstered stools worshippers kneel on during church services). Two seminal texts for Clare, as for so many working-class readers, were *The Pilgrim's Progress* and *Robinson Crusoe*, and both are glanced at here: the quagmire is a version of the Slough of Despond, while the theme of anxiety ('fear encamps') coupled with that of island solitude is Crusoe's. The 'hassock tufts' are also graves in a country churchyard, because Clare is drawing on that great democratic poem, Gray's 'Elegy in a Country Churchyard,' which states 'Some mute inglorious Milton here may rest'. The snipe 'alone and mute' is Clare alluding both to Gray and by extension Milton, and to the dumbness which his social position as an agricultural day labourer nearly forced on him, but which he is conquering by speaking out in poems. He has moved from provincial dumbness to metropolitan eloquence (his first volume, *Poems Descriptive of Rural Life and Scenery*, was published in 1820). But he fears that the fashion for poetry written by 'a peasant', as he was styled on the title page of that volume, will change – as it did – and he will be rendered dumb again.

That word 'mute' is both isolated and under the pressure of enjambment – it must carry across into the next line and over the stanza break. This isolates and emphasises it, rather as the assonance in 'home alone' isolates that phrase. The word 'mute' echoes and reverberates through the poem – *good rude solitude spews moors hugh muse woods foot food chuse suited look* – and we may note that the first *m* in swamps gathers in the opening lines until it puts an emphasis on the initial *m* in 'man', which is then made even stronger when we reach 'mute'. Clare was a gifted fiddler and, like Burns, a collector of traditional songs – his ear is very delicate, as well as subtly allusive.

The assonantal *oo* pattern expresses the poem's ontological anxiety, which is also present in the phrase 'fear encamps' (there was an army camp nearby and Clare had enlisted in the militia). The quaking trembling grass, the 'fowl that dread', 'dreaded sight' and 'skulking fowler' deepen and extend this pervasive angst. The word 'invest' suggests both a siege and economic investment, while the phrase 'spa-red water spews' brings in both class and military struggle, as well as that bad-taste theme Clare employs to create an unsettling dissonance.

The hard rhyme *clump/stump* in the third stanza suggests 'thump', while the willow stump suggests a dismembered body, as 'sallow' puns on the adjective describing an unpleasantly white or yellow complexion (it is cognate with the French word for 'dirty', *sale*). In mentioning the willow, Clare is remembering Psalm 137, where 'We hanged our hopes upon the willows', and where the psalmist asks 'How shall we sing the Lord's song in a strange land?' Clare did an imitation of that psalm, writing:

> Our harps upon the willows hung
>   Cares silenced every string
> Our woes unheeded & unsung
>   No hearts we have to sing

The loss and desolation of the psalm is implicit in the 'old sallow stump'.

But the mood lifts in the next stanza with that rare and unexpected verb 'hilling', though 'rancid' deliberately skews this effect and prepares the way for another unexpected Latinate adjective, 'gelid', in the next stanza, which is packed with *d* sounds. The word 'rude' was a favourite with Clare (he uses it over 260 times in his poems), and it contains another allusion to Gray's Elegy: 'Each in his narrow cell for ever laid/ The rude forefathers of the hamlet sleep.' The snipe's bill is a symbol of Clare's rude peasant pen, what he elsewhere calls his 'jobbling pen' – a pun on 'jobbing' and 'hobbling'. But the word 'rude' has contradictory meanings in English: we speak of 'rude good health', and in Black English 'a rude boy' is a term of respect. As Clare uses 'rude' in his poems, it is a nodal or complex word which fathers many associations and meanings. Spelt 'rood' it is Anglo-Saxon for 'cross', and the churchyard theme abets this. The word 'bill' also means 'pike', the weapon, and the fact that it can both 'delve and drill' echoes a piece of medieval popular verse from the Peasants' Revolt: 'When Adam dalf and Eve span/ Who was then the gentleman?' The bill is both spade and pen, but it can also be a pike, a weapon, just as 'drill' can be a military term. The internal rhyme *good/rude* makes the latter adjective lose its pejorative meanings, a process that *food* completes.

Then something strange happens, as Clare drops in the rather precious adjective 'gelid', which carries a memory of 'rancid' in the previous stanza. Goldsmith speaks of gales expanding their 'gelid Wings', Marvell mentions gelid strawberries, meaning they are cold and refreshing, but Clare's gelid is also ugly, mushy, uncomfortable. It chimes with 'tepid' and with that rare, lovely adjective 'trepid'. These are words that belong to confident, classical English, though 'trepid' (line 67) has an exquisite, justifiably self-conscious and surprising air about it, which sets it apart.

That sound is dry in contrast to the boggy, sinky, squelchy landscape, which is vulnerable to rapacious 'free booters' who bring dread and death into it. Yet to call this a landscape is to appropriate and command it in a rather eighteenth-century, upper-class manner. This is wilderness, an asocial terrain penetrated by men, but also possessed of a visionary dreariness and creative solitariness that evades and escapes them. With its howling tempests and naked exposure, this is also Lear's heath – and the bird's 'mystic nest' even glances at Shakespeare's 'The Phoenix and the Turtle', though there is no allusive verbal link. There is an allusion to Milton near the end, though, in 'that creep or walk or flye', as Clare indents his 'cordial' benign respect for insects, birds and reptiles with a memory of Satan as he 'swims or sinks, or wades, or creeps, or flies' in *Paradise Lost.* Charles Lamb said that Clare transplanted Arcadia to Helpston, but he also transfers the hellish bog Satan is crossing to Emmonsales Heath. In the word 'creep' there is also a memory of the first chapter of Genesis, where God gives to Man dominion over 'every creeping thing that creepeth upon the earth'. The religious context gives the final stanza a pious, liturgical tone where 'Thine' at the beginning of the last stanza could be addressed to God as Clare offers his desolate, passive acceptance of things as they are. His ear in the last stanza is almost tormented by a series of *ee* sounds which take on a dull sadness in *meanest creep dreariest* until 'peace will be' redeems them and prepares the way for the last line.

Gray's Elegy ends with an epitaph, which begins 'Here rests his head upon this lap of earth,/ A youth to fortune and to fame unknown', and Clare's phrase 'The moors desolate and spungy lap' picks up that 'lap of earth' as well as repeating 'rude' and so underlining the allusion to the Elegy. Gray also speaks of 'this neglected spot', and Clare's *lot spot plot not* draw 'spot' out in order to emphasise its dreariness and ugliness. It's almost like the 'damned spot' in *Macbeth.* That hard dental *d* is there in the penultimate line's 'dreariest', which carries 'mans dreaded sight', and in 'dread man's sight', as well as many other words with *d* in them. But the sound's final impact is on 'dweller' in the last line, which gains lift-off because it contains 'well' inside – a word which means both the opposite of 'ill' and an often holy place where sweet water can be drawn. This prepares us for 'joy', which seems to fly up and away to join 'employ'.

Central to the anguish in this poem is Enclosure, which robbed Clare and his community of their access to common land and to the medieval strip system of agriculture's open-field landscape.

Lord Byron ~ from *Don Juan*

Now overhead a rainbow, bursting through
  The scattering clouds, shone, spanning the dark sea,
Resting its bright base on the quivering blue;
  And all within its arch appear'd to be
Clearer than that without, and its wide hue
  Wax'd broad and waving, like a banner free,
Then changed like to a bow that's bent, and then
Forsook the dim eyes of these shipwreck'd men.

It changed, of course; a heavenly cameleon,
  The airy child of vapour and the sun,
Brought forth in purple, cradled in vermilion,
  Baptized in molten gold, and swathed in dun,
Glittering like crescents o'er a Turk's pavilion,
  And blending every colour into one,
Just like a black eye in a recent scuffle,
(For sometimes we must box without the muffle).

[Canto 2, 92–3]

Byron's verse leaps – those *ee* sounds in the opening line and a half of the second stanza make it feel agile, joyous, exultant, as he describes a rainbow early in *Don Juan*. The chameleon in the second stanza seems to leap like a chamois, the little Alpine goatlike animal prized by the Romantics and often mistaken for a type of deer. Wordsworth invokes it as he climbs the Cumberland mountains in *The Prelude*, and Hazlitt compares the nimbleness of Burke's prose style to it. But 'chameleon', the shape-changer, has 'sham' and 'me' inside it, and Byron's eye for the bogus, his intense awareness that he is going to make a great deal of money from his comic epic, and his knowledge of his own poses and changing identities, all touch on this self-referring pun. He mocks this when he says:

> And though these lines should only line portmanteaus,
> Trade will be all the better for these cantos.

With savage wit, he makes a similar point when he describes Don Juan caught up in a battle:

> And as he rushed along, it came to pass he
> Fell in with what was late the second column,
> Under the orders of the General Lascy,
> But now reduced, as is a bulky volume
> Into an elegant extract (much less massy)
> Of heroism, and took his place with solemn
> Air 'midst the rest, who kept their valiant faces
> And levelled weapons still against the glacis.

In this period, there was a well-known anthology compiled by the Reverend Vicesimus Knox that was called *Elegant Extracts of Poetry Selected for the Improvement of Young Persons.* Byron's savage joke merges culture and barbarism.

He knows that he is going to have fun rhyming 'chameleon', because from 'vermilion' to 'pavilion' he is able to strike out at the Prince Regent's Brighton Pavilion. He spells out its extravagant cost in a later stanza – 'Shut up – no, not the King, but the Pavilion,/ Or else 'twill cost us all another million'.

That word 'million' which lies inside *chameleon/vermilion* brings society into the sunset, and draws it away from being a natural phenomenon to something that is in advanced bad taste – the bright purple, the vermilion and gold demonstrate this, while that boring colour 'dun', which has an extra rhyme with 'pavilion', punningly brings debt into the image, and so undermines the pavilion. A child is being born here, a gifted child who might be a figure for the future heroic poet and liberator.

The Romantic poet is swathed in ridiculous colours, and the language is both poetic and the opposite of poetic – 'of course' belongs to confident conversation, as does the adjective 'heavenly'. Byron wants his verse always to have the pitch and variety of familiar conversation: 'And never straining hard to versify,/ I rattle on exactly as I'd talk/ With anybody in a ride or walk.' Open, frank conversation, he's saying, is an Englishman's right. Like William Cobbett, he's going to speak the truth and be damned. This means that there is a dramatic tension in the poem between its tight verse form – ottava rima (ABABABCC) – and the spontaneity of its conversational wit and energy.

He reflects on this early in the poem:

> I don't know that there may be much ability
>   Shown in this sort of desultory rhyme,
> But there's a conversational facility,
>   Which may round off an hour upon a time.
> Of this I'm sure at least, there's no servility
>   In mine irregularity of chime,
> Which rings what's uppermost of new or hoary,
>   Just as I feel the *improvvisatore.*

That rhyme and metre can be desultory, boring, shop-soiled, cheap, offensive and servile is a running theme in *Don Juan*. Byron turns on the poetry of his society, rhyming Southey with 'mouthy', and dismissing a 'drowsy frowzy poem called the *Excursion*/ Writ in a manner which is my aversion'. By referring to his 'ingenuity of chime', and in a later deliberately scratchy, comic, Russian stanza to his 'discords of narration', he insists that his subjects – war, history, politics – will not be tested in verse that is 'smooth as Rogers' rhymes' (a swipe at the banker poet, Samuel Rogers).

He wants us to pay attention to vocal passages and changes in tone, and here the parenthesis is vital to the smart effects he seeks. Thus his reference to Rogers is an aside in a moment of comic narrative, as Donna Julia's jealous husband and servants batter down her bedroom door:

> Their duty was – for they were strong and though
> They looked so little, did strong things at times –
> To ope this door, which they could really do
> (The hinges being as smooth as Rogers' rhymes),

Byron now combines the parenthesis with a perfectly-timed pause after 'chaste', when he turns to Juan's married lover:

> Julia (whom on this occasion
> I shall have much to speak about), and she
> Was married, charming, chaste, and twenty-three.

That last adjective after the pause at 'chaste' wittily unsettles the conventional and superficial adjectives that precede it. This use of the pause is naturally buoyed by the caesura in the heavenly chameleon stanza, and its erotic, suggestive meaning is felt in the lines about Julia, as well as in 'I'm fond of fire, and crickets, and all that, /A lobster salad, and champagne, and chat.'

Sometimes Byron will put a pause inside a closing rhyme, to still the moment as he stretches a sound to make what is called a 'synthetic rhyme'. Most brilliantly, he does it in this couplet:

> I pass my evenings in long galleries solely,
> And that's the reason I'm so melancholy.

Here, his camp wit makes the natural sound and rhythm of 'melancholy' – that Romantic value – suddenly become richly artificial, as a self-consciously drawn-out theatrical voice completes the rhyme. Again, this is a form of camp, as when he transforms the clouds at sunset into showy colours that glitter like crescents over a Turk's pavilion. But not content with this, he takes the image back to nature by converting it into a black eye received by a pugilist. He has moved from royalty to the people, and has brought the sweat and violence and betting of the crowd into the poem. That technical term 'muffle' shows that Byron knows about pugilism and low life, and is one of the many moments in the poem which act to deflate a pretentious or elite poetic language. In a sense, this is an image of coming revolution, of violence that is still to happen. No wonder this was a favourite poem with British working-class radicals. But from the heavenly chameleon in the first line to the muffle at the end of the last, there is a bathetic effect, which has the paradoxical purpose of making the heroic poet figure with his changing identities assume the identity of a tough boxer, a lord who can use what was called 'flash language' – the slang of racecourses and boxing rings.

The gutturals that begin with 'cradle' place a strong emphasis on 'bow', which halts the line for a moment. The guttural is carried over into the opening line of the next stanza – 'Our shipwrecked seamen thought it a good omen' – and it is also huskily present in that stanza's concluding couplet: 'and so this rainbow looked like hope,/Quite a celestial kaleidoscope.' That last word has 'celestial' as well as 'chameleon' and its rhymes inside it, so that it acquires the *haeccitas*, the density, of a physical object. Byron's rhymes are fun because they are so tactile, so sensuous. He is, as he described himself, 'the grand Napoleon of the realms of rhyme'.

Robert Browning ~ 'Meeting at Night'

I

The grey sea and the long black land;
And the yellow half-moon large and low;
And the startled little waves that leap
In fiery ringlets from their sleep,
As I gain the cove with pushing prow,
And quench its speed i' the slushy sand.

II

Then a mile of warm sea-scented beach;
Three fields to cross till a farm appears;
A tap at the pane, the quick sharp scratch
And blue spurt of a lighted match,
And a voice less loud, thro' its joys and fears,
Than the two hearts beating each to each!

The metre of this almost perfect poem shifts line by line:

The grey sea/ and the/ long black land;
And the/ yellow/ half-moon/ large and low

It pays out those *l*s, erotic sounds that suggest lovers' kisses and, some might say, lust. The *ar* sound in 'large' is picked up by 'startled', so that its first syllable brings 'star' somewhere into play – the repeated sound makes the syllable stand out and detach itself slightly from the word. The *uh* in 'large' travels down to 'slushy', so that syllable is ever so slightly arrested before the word completes itself. The internal rhyme *yellow/low* in the second line builds the yellow moon, which is half-complete like the speaker's love, as he looks forward to hugging his woman. It must be a crescent moon growing like his desire. The word 'low' is perhaps a slight joke at the low subject of the poem – sexual desire – and the low people it contains. I wonder if this is the first poem with a safety match in it? Browning is the master of this type of detail – a Defoe-like poet, an unrelenting realist.

The little waves become 'fiery ringlets', a figure for her slightly dishevelled hair, which is drawing fire and passion from the moonlight and from his fantasy of their meeting. It is her being 'startled' that he is imagining – this is less the pathetic fallacy than his fantasy of her. The fact that this is to be a nocturnal meeting suggests something covert, even underhand. In 'leap' we have his fantasy of her leaping out of bed when he knocks on the windowpane – an action that can't be portrayed in verse without crossing certain Victorian boundaries of good taste. The words 'leap' and 'sleep' form a couplet rhyme, a kiss, an embrace – the first and last lines are kept far apart, the next two closer, the next pair closest.

The word 'cove' takes emphasis because it reflects 'yellow' and 'low', which brings their *ls* to make *love* somewhere in the word. The word 'gain' is acquisitive, male, and the whole line capable of being a double entendre. From the *g* in 'ringlets' to 'gain,' to 'cove,' to 'quench', the gutturals are building. The 'pushing prow' is phallic, as the 'slushy sand' is vaginal (it contains 'lush'), and the prow moves intently forward unimpeded by having to rhyme (there is only an eye rhyme with 'low'). But perhaps the richest word is 'quench', which picks up the *k* in 'cove'. It's guttural like 'scratch'. We extinguish or quench fire, a blacksmith cools red hot metal by quenching it in water, we quench desire and motion and thirst. The word reverberates with heat and desire, and sets up what is still to happen.

He can smell her warm, sleepy body in the warm 'sea-scented beach', and in that last faint *ch*, we hear before it happens 'scratch' and 'match', as well as the paired rhyme words 'beach' and 'each', like the soft smack of kisses. But we also at some level realise that the sea scent is salt – it's as though he can smell his sperm already staining the bedsheet, its fishy salty smell. We also hear the *ch* sound, in 'quench', as the *ee* in sea joins the *ee* in 'beach'.

Now the scrape of heavy wood on sand is echoed by an ordinary but miraculous moment when, after his finger taps the pane, the head of the match is drawn down the sandpaper. This is the fire of passion, the spurt of male orgasm, the quick of life, but she is in control here. Having coded intense longing and desire to this point, the poem has nowhere else to go. The last couplet is conventional, the emotions too general, so that the final exclamation disappoints. This poem, short and beautiful as it is, cannot sustain itself beyond the epiphany of the lighted match.

Alfred, Lord Tennyson ~ from *In Memoriam*

VII

Dark house, by which once more I stand
  Here in the long unlovely street,
  Doors, where my heart was used to beat
So quickly, waiting for a hand,

A hand that can be clasped no more –
  Behold me, for I cannot sleep,
  And like a guilty thing I creep
At earliest morning to the door.

He is not here; but far away
  The noise of life begins again,
  And ghastly through the drizzling rain
On the bald street breaks the blank day.

vii 7. *And*] But *H.MS.* Cp. the ghost in *Hamlet* I i 148: 'And then it started like a guilty thing'. Also Wordsworth's *Immortality Ode* 148–5: (note the subject, and 'blank'): 'Blank misgivings of a Creature/ Moving about in worlds not realised,/ High instincts before which our mortal Nature/ Did tremble like a guilty Thing surprised.'
vii 9. J. D. Rosenberg, *JEGP* lviii (1959) 230, suggests an allusion to *Luke* xxiv 6, with the angel before the empty sepulchre: 'He is not here, but is risen'.
vii 11. *drizzling*] dripping *H. MS.*

I've taken this text from Christopher Ricks's great edition of Tennyson. Ricks's notes illuminate this lyric, which is the subtlest in the sequence, both in rhythm and imaginative depth. Tennyson's gifted friend Arthur Hallam died in Vienna at the age of twenty-two. Tennyson began writing the poem in 1833, the year Hallam died, finished it in 1850, and published the sequence of elegies anonymously the following year. Here, he revisits the London street, Wimpole Street, where Hallam lived with his family.

The 'dark house' is the body and contains a memory of Dante's 'selva oscura' (dark wood) at the beginning of *The Divine Comedy* – Hallam was a gifted Italian scholar and would have appreciated the reference to the phrase, which occurs in the second line of Dante's epic. Tennyson must begin the poem with *d*, the hard unyielding death sound, which is there too in the last word, 'day'. Also, by beginning the poem with a spondee – 'Dārk hoūse' – he isolates and stops the line short, and this looks forward to the doubly spondaic last line. The dark house is like a tomb; it is abandoned, sinister, threatening. That phrase 'once more' picks up the most famous, most quoted elegy in English – Milton's *Lycidas*, which begins: 'Yet once more, O ye laurels, and once more / Ye myrtles brown, with ivy never sere'. That *w* in 'once' picks up and amplifies the *w* in 'which' immediately before it to make an ugly, uncomfortable sound. Then Tennyson does something slightly odd, by calling the street 'unlovely', rather than ugly. The word brings love and no love immediately into the poem, but there is a slightly camp quality to the word; or perhaps it acquired such a quality near the end of the nineteenth century, when Oscar Wilde in the dock referred to 'a most unlovely boy'? There is a homoerotic texture to this and some of the other lyrics in the sequence, but it skews the poem to inflect 'unlovely' in a Wildean tone. Its double *l* sound picks up 'long' and this suggests 'lips', suggests the wish to return kisses. There is a traditional phrase for death – 'gone to his long home' – and that idea is also present in 'long'. Tennyson is also introducing the first molossus in 'lōng ūnlōve', which counterpoints the iambic rhythm. Tennyson's ear is running with the guttural *k* in 'Dark', and he repeats it in 'quickly', which brings the word 'life' to mind, as in the phrase 'the quick and the dead'. The quick of highly sensitive feeling is present in the adverb, which passes that guttural *k* sound onto 'clasped', which is almost masonic in its masculinity (Tennyson and Hallam belonged to the elite Cambridge undergraduate society known as the Apostles). The *k* sound is also picked up in the last line's 'blank'.

Ricks's note explains the clever double allusion in 'guilty thing', a phrase which makes Tennyson into a surrogate ghost. But this is also a homoerotic moment, where Tennyson is likening himself to a betrayed woman who, in a typical Victorian novel or melodrama, is returning to her former lover's house. It's common in religious poetry for the soul to be imaged as a female, God as a harsh male lover. Donne uses this traditional trope, and so does Hopkins when he compares his prayers to letters 'sent to dearest him that lives alas! Away'. This is a type of bereaved cross-dressing – imagining his male grief and vulnerability as female – and it expresses the anger he feels towards his friend for dying.

Then in a note gleaned from the *Journal of English and Germanic Philology*, we notice the cunning allusion to the empty sepulchre in Luke, an almost invisible gesture which transforms Hallam into Christ. It's now that we are able to see how all the complicated, contradictory feelings in this brief lyric bear down on that apparently innocuous semi-colon in line 9. Hearing the poem read aloud, the line becomes 'He is not here, but far away'. In the printed text we read 'He is not here. But far away/ The noise of life begins again,' but even here the pause at 'away' keeps the possibility open of Hallam being alive somewhere else – a common feeling in bereavement. It's a subliminally aural effect, which introduces a kind of hope that is immediately cancelled by the last two lines. This is the Victorian view of the material world – dead, inert, spiritless, but with a faintly Wordsworthian pantheism still clinging to the word 'blank'.

In another note, Ricks points to the similarity of line 4 to the third line in this lyric:

> Break, break, break
> On thy cold grey stones, O sea,
> But O for the touch of a vanished hand
> That never comes back to me.

This helps us hear how Tennyson's ear is caught by 'dark' and 'break'. He is remembering Milton's lines in *Samson Agonistes*:

> O dark, dark, dark, amid the blaze of noon,
> Irrecoverably dark, total eclipse
> Without all hope of day!

The rhythm of 'Break, break, break' is torn between the first line's three strong stresses and the facile anapaestic movement of 'But O for the touch of a vanished hand'. Something similar happens in *In Memoriam* VII, which is written in regular iambic tetrameters:

> The noise/ of life/ begins/again

before that rhythm is smashed by:

> On the bald street breaks the blank day.

The spondees in the second and last foot have the effect of a spanner being thrown into the smoothly functioning iambic meter of the previous lines. It is as though Tennyson has anticipated Verlaine's advice to wring rhetoric's neck. The hard alliterative rhythm comes fighting out of Old and Middle English poetry to wreck the elocutionary smoothness of the rest of the poem.

The ghostly guilty thing alluded to in the second stanza returns in 'ghastly', so that the material world appears to dissolve into a visionary phantasmagoria whose abstract materiality denies religious vision. Those two guttural *k*s in 'breaks' and 'blank' give it a rough texture, as though it can be grasped, not like a living hand, but a heavy, ice-cold, dead hand. The last line wrecks everything that has gone before – it is almost as though he is witnessing not the dawn, but a terrible accident that repeats the death of his beloved friend.

Emily Dickinson ~ 'He fumbles at your Soul'

He fumbles at your Soul
As Players at the Keys
Before they drop full Music on –
He stuns you by degrees –
Prepares your brittle Nature
For the Ethereal Blow
By fainter Hammers – further heard –
Then nearer – Then so slow
Your Breath has time to straighten –
Your Brain – to bubble Cool -
Deals – One – imperial – Thunderbolt –
That scalps your naked Soul –

When Winds take Forests in their Paws –
The Universe – is still –

Again and again, Dickinson is drawn to the erotic, but in this poem she is suspicious of a masculine use of sexual attraction and of female response to it. Here, I take it, she is writing about a preacher who uses a well-known rhetorical technique to set his audience at ease before he really gets into his sermon. Perhaps he says something casual in a soft, gentle voice, perhaps he makes a few announcements – a vestry meeting, a sale to raise funds for the church. He needs to get his congregation into the palm of his hand, and that is not done, at least initially, by raising his voice. He knows that it sometimes relaxes an audience to begin clumsily, maybe by tripping over your words, even dropping something by deliberate mistake on the floor.

Dickinson means all this by the word 'fumble'. And she means more, because in her mind's eye she can see a man's hand trying to undo a woman's bodice. The action is clumsy, ugly, dominant, intrusive. He wants to hold your soul in his power and shape it, even destroy it by robbing it of its freedom. This is power and authority exercised by an individual who is intent on subordinating other free individual consciences to his authority. The image for this is what can serve as a warming-up process for a concert audience – a pianist is idly running their hands over the keyboard before starting to play. The word 'drop' is ominous – we're not far from a trapdoor in the floor of a gallows here. At some level, all performers have to fool – i.e. persuade – their audience, so there may be a pun on 'full'. The close assonance in 'fūll Mūsic' is attractive – those *oo* sounds – but that sensuousness may hint at deception, a kind of siren song.

The *uh* sound in 'stuns' picks up the ugly *uh* sound in fumbles', but the nasal *n* is harder and cleaner than the labial *m*. The verb 'stuns' seems to replicate 'drop', because both are vigorous monosyllables and carry violence. Dickinson is communicating how the apparently unstudied action of a pianist before a recital is deceptive, like the apparently clumsy beginning of the preacher's performance, a performance which is in fact deft, professional, continued. The preacher's introductory words are disarmingly casual and aim to lull the audience.

There is a contradiction here: you cannot stun a living creature by degrees, it is not a gradual process. The idea is that a premeditated casualness can enlist sympathy in an audience, and once that receptive sympathy is there the orator can start to completely mesmerise the audience. Behind 'stuns' is the image of an animal in an abattoir being stunned before having its throat cut. The seduction is both gradual and deadly, as 'degrees' takes on the weight of 'drops'. The violation that is taking place is a form of spiritual murder – what would be the actual murder of a high-born woman in a

Jacobean tragedy. There is a curiously similar moment in Henry James's *Washington Square*, when Catherine Sloper fears that her tyrannical father is trying to destroy her, body and soul, as they argue in a cold Alpine valley: 'There was a kind of still intensity about her father which made him dangerous, but Catherine hardly went so far as to say to herself that it might be part of his plan to fasten his hand – the neat, fine, supple hand of a distinguished physician – in her throat.' Here the free female spirit struggles with a murderous patriarch.

The New England Puritanism which shaped Dickinson's imagination, as it shaped James's, asserts the primacy of the individual conscience, the free spirit, over all controlling authorities. In Dickinson's poem, authority enforces itself through a gradual stunning process that is both soothing and playful. This sinister seduction combines the concert/sermon figure with the idea of entering an abattoir, a blacksmith's forge or a church where a marriage will take place. Perhaps the blacksmith is a figure for the god, Vulcan, who is then a figure for the wrath of the Old Testament? So you are the bride being prepared for the 'Ethereal Blow', the heavenly hammer blow that is marriage in a church to a man in a ceremony presided over by a male priest. But really, both male figures combine: he is burglar/blacksmith/bridegroom, a version of the line in another of her love lyrics – 'Burglar, Banker, Father'.

It's at this point that the frequency and pace of the dashes increases as the poem begins almost to break up under the pressure of his rhetoric. The hammer implicit in 'stuns' becomes the little wooden hammers in a piano as the crescendo increases and, we assume, a long dramatic pause follows. It's here that the physical metaphor of straightening your breath suggests the act of adjusting one's dress, disturbed by his groping, fumbling hand. Then she introduces the blacksmith image in 'bubble cool', which echoes back to 'full Music' and so contradicts the idea of coolness. It's as if the brain, like red hot metal, is forever seething as it hits cold water.

This is an image of the vehement, volcanic puritan spirit controlled by male power.

Then the male figure becomes Zeus, all powerful, as he deals a thunderbolt like a blow – a metaphor that takes us back to 'the Ethereal Blow'. His hand on your hair is like a native American preparing to scalp you as you stand naked before him – ancient anxieties, bits of history and folklore are shaping this moment, but the man's hand on the woman's hair is somewhere the image of the seducer's hand grasping or stroking her pubic hair.

That 'Thunderbolt' picks up 'stuns'. Against that masculine sound is set the gendered adjective 'brittle', which functions rather like the phrase 'dimity Convictions' in another of her lyrics. She is severe on women, at least on traditional women, and lets the windstorm give way to the peace that follows orgasm. The combination of blacksmith, tiger, hammer and forests points to Blake, who has 'forests of the night' in 'The Tiger'. Like Blake, Dickinson gives certain psychological states a visionary force in which the terms of the sublime reflect both the individual psyche and the social world, where violence and cruelty abound. She is alive to the fascination which power exerts, and believes it is permanent, universal, unchangeable, as if we are condemned to make our fantasies real. Where the tiger symbolises revolution in Blake, this lyric critically represents the consuming force of evangelical Protestantism in American culture.

Christina Rossetti ~ 'Margaret has a milking-pail' and excerpt from *Goblin Market*

Margaret has a milking-pail,
And she rises early;
Thomas has a threshing-flail,
And he's up betimes.

Sometimes crossing through the grass
Where the dew lies pearly,
They say 'Good-morrow' as they pass
By the leafy limes.

~

'Good folk,' said Lizzie,
Mindful of Jeanie:
'Give me much and many:' –
Held out her apron,
Tossed them her penny.
'Nay, take a seat with us,
Honour and eat with us:'
They answered grinning:
'Our feast is but beginning.
Night yet is early,
Warm and dew-pearly,
Wakeful and starry:
Such fruits as these
No man can carry;
Half their bloom would fly,
Half their dew would dry,
Half their flavour would pass by.
Sit down and feast with us,

Be welcome guest with us,
Cheer you and rest with us.' –
'Thank you,' said Lizzie.: 'But one waits
At home alone for me:
So without further parleying,
If you will not sell me any
Of your fruits tho' much and many,
Give me back my silver penny
I tossed you for a fee.' –
They began to scratch their pates,
No longer wagging, purring,
But visibly demurring,
Grunting and snarling.
One called her proud,
Cross-grained, uncivil;
Their tones waxed loud,
Their looks were evil.
Lashing their tails
They trod and hustled her,
Elbowed and jostled her,
Clawed with their nails,
Barking, mewing, hissing, mocking,
Tore her gown and soiled her stocking,
Twitched her hair out by the roots,
Stamped upon her tender feet,
Held her hands and squeezed their fruits
Against her mouth to make her eat.
White and golden Lizzie stood,
Like a lily in a flood, –
Like a rock of blue-veined stone
Lashed by tides obstreperously, –
Like a beacon left alone
In a hoary roaring sea,

Sending up a golden fire, –
Like a fruit-crowned orange-tree
White with blossoms honey-sweet
Sore beset by wasp and bee, –
Like a royal virgin town
Topped with gilded dome and spire
Close beleaguered by a fleet
Mad to tug her standard down.

This simple poem is subtle and sinister. It is the *l*s that carry uneasy resonance. They are innocent in 'milking-pail' and 'early', but when they reappear twice in 'flail' they are associated with a masculine object which is a type of weapon. This complicates 'pearly' in a line which is not far off a version of the foggy, foggy dew of ballads – a figure for sperm (a necklace of pearls is a politer image).

The two *l*s thean reappear in 'leafy limes', which combine trees with what in *Goblin Market* would be a tempting fruit. Maybe one day they'll go into the wood? What will happen there?

Christina Rossetti published *Goblin Market* in 1862. With *The Wreck of the Deutschland,* it is one of the greatest achievements of Victorian poetry – it has a subtlety of rhythm and cadence, as well as a shifting, ambiguous subject, which exerted an enormous influence on English poetry. Rossetti will not allow one line to sound like another, so she varies pitch, stress, metre, mixing short two-beat lines with longer lines. The rhythm changes constantly.

Some of Rossetti's contemporaries did not share an admiration for her command of poetic rhythm. They could not understand her need to vary line length and rhythm. Ruskin said that her poems were full of 'quaintnesses and offences', and added that irregular measure was 'the calamity of modern poetry', because it violated the 'common ear for metre'. He told Dante Gabriel Rossetti, 'your sister should exercise herself in the severest commonplaces of metre until she can write as the public like'.

Dante Gabriel Rossetti objected to what he called the 'metrical jolt' in her poem 'The Prince's Progress', and advised her not to publish her complex religious and feminist poem 'The Iniquity of the Fathers'. Her poems were seen as being full of 'harsh discords', or as 'simply execrable'. Hopkins and Swinburne recognised a new poetic, and wrote admiringly of her in their letters. Rossetti's metric, they realised, was based on the subtle, changing contours of the speaking voice, its spontaneity and intimacy.

Like Hopkins, she looked to nursery and skipping rhymes for the deep structures of the oral language, and in 1872 she published *Sing-Song, a Nursery Rhyme Book*. It contains the short, apparently innocent lyric, printed above the excerpt from *Goblin Market*, where Rossetti returns to her theme in that poem of violent male sexuality. The combination of the plosive *p* and *ail* in the first line of 'Margaret has a milking-pail' begins a fine subliminal anxiety. She is not asking, like Keats, 'Oh, what can ail thee, knight-at-arms?', though she, too, is telling a story of boy meets girl. In her poem nothing happens, but something could or may be about to happen. Her ear is running with those liquid *l*s, which begin with 'pail' and culminate in the leafy limes. They also occur twice in 'flail', which is a weapon used to thresh grain.

The image of pearly dew is a version of the foggy foggy dew found in many traditional songs of sex and betrayal – the string of pearls is its more polite equivalent (the plosive *p* in 'pearly' picks up 'pail'). This symbolism and the *flail/pail* rhyme are a version of Jack and Jill going up the hill to fetch a pail of water. The equivalent intimacy of Margaret and Thomas is shadowed in both an erotic and sinister fashion by those two *l*s in the last line. The leafy limes are tempting and dangerous.

That danger pervades *Goblin Market*, where the goblin men hustle Lizzie and try to break her will, like the bearded Victorian patriarchs they represent. Their violence is embedded in trochaic verse:

> Barking, mewing, hissing, mocking,
> Tore her gown and soiled her stocking,
> Twitched her hair out by the roots.

She breaks with this trochaic rhythm as the next line progresses: 'Stamped upon her tender feet'. This changed rhythm designs a pause, a return to normative metre, before she picks up the trochaic rhythm again and applies its strength to Lizzie:

> White and golden Lizzie stood,
> Like a lily in the flood, –
> Like a rock of blue-veined stone.

Lizzie is a pure virgin, who is given the Virgin Mary's colours. But the rhythm is subtly different, because that blue-veined stone is a molossus, whose three strong stresses formidably arrest the line and make it even stronger, weightier.

The image perhaps goes in different directions: on the one hand it is catholic and aristocratic, implying Lizzie has blue blood. On the other hand by linking 'blue' with 'veined', Rossetti may be remembering a rather shocking line from Browning's 'The Bishop Orders his Tomb at St Praxed's Church' in which the dying lecher relishes a lump of lapis lazuli 'Blue as a vein o'er the Madonna's breast'. If she is remembering Browning's line, it is because her feelings about Catholicism are hostile (she was a devout Anglican), and she is also touching on the theme of male sexuality here. Bt she is also asserting a firm female purity.

The lash of the tides brings back the 'flail' in the other poem, and the adverb 'obstreperously' is masculine (it contains both 'strap' and 'strop', as well as male anger). Lizzie firmly resists this power, and the *o* in 'golden' travels down to 'stone' and 'alone', then to 'dome' and 'close', to design a circular fort against the angry waves.

Rossetti rhymes on this sound in her poem 'Enrica', where she contrasts the 'liberal glow' of a visiting cousin from Italy, with her and her sisters:

> We Englishwomen, trim, correct,
>   All minted in the selfsame mould,
>   Warm-hearted but of semblance cold,
> All courteous out of self-respect.

She then introduces a maritime image, as she does in the passage from *Goblin Market*:

> But if she found us like our sea,
>   Of aspect colourless and chill,
>   Rock-girt; like it she found us still
> Deep at our deepest, strong and free.

Here, she asserts England as a free Protestant nation against Italy's Catholicism and political subjection. In the passage from *Goblin Market*, she doesn't quite use 'free', which is implicit in 'sea', except the sea is male power here, so 'tyranny' is also implicit.

The beacon is a particularly Protestant image, a version of Milton's lonely tower with its midnight lamp – the free individual conscience – and a memory of the beacons that were lit along the coast of England to warn of the approach of the Spanish Armada. Famously, Queen Elizabeth said in a speech to her troops and sailors at Tilbury on the approach of the Armada:

> I know I have the body of a weak and feeble woman, but I have the heart and stomach of a King, and a King of England too; and think foul scorn that Parma or Spain should dare to invade the borders of my realm.

In designing an image of female fortitude, Rossetti draws on Elizabeth's speech.

The word 'hoary', though it describes the whiteness of foam and surf, also puns on a reality Rossetti knew well from her charity work with reformed prostitutes at a home in Highgate. Here, she glances at the victims of the roaring sea. Then, after repeating 'golden', she balances the earlier Catholic blue with its complimentary colour, orange. Partly, she is recalling these lines in George Herbert's 'Employment', where he exclaims: 'Oh that I were an Orange-tree/ That busy plant!' But she also knows that the colour carries an inescapable association with England's Calvinist king, William of Orange, so that the two colours together create an image of that *via media*, the Church of England. The molossus 'blūe-vēined stōne' is repeated in 'frūit-crōwned ōrăngе', like either side of an arch.

She then repeats the virginal white, before introducing the phallic wasps and bees, who are intent on invading Lizzie's realm, like the fleet closing in on her. The sexual violence in the last line threatens her autonomy and virginity, both of which are symbolised by the flag that also represents national sovereignty. The word 'standard' naturally implies 'moral standard', as the brutal and immoral goblins close in on her. They fail and the poem ends happily. It is a unique achievement, which endlessly eludes its interpreters.

G. M. Hopkins ~ 'That Nature Is a Heraclitean Fire and of the Comfort of the Resurrection'

Cloud-puffball, torn tufts, tossed pillows | flaunt forth, then chevy on an air-
built thoroughfare: heaven-roysterers, in gay-gangs | they throng; they glitter in marches.
Down roughcast, down dazzling whitewash, | wherever an elm arches,
Shivelights and shadowtackle in long | lashes lace, lance, and pair.
Delightfully the bright wind boisterous | ropes, wrestles, beats earth bare
Of yestertempest's creases; | in pool and rutpeel parches
Squandering ooze to squeezed | dough, crust, dust; stanches, starches
Squadroned masks and manmarks | treadmire toil there
Footfretted in it. Million-fuelèd, | nature's bonfire burns on.
But quench her bonniest, dearest | to her, her clearest-selvèd spark
Man, how fast his firedint, | his mark on mind, is gone!
Both are in an unfathomable, all is in an enormous dark
Drowned. O pity and indig | nation! Manshape, that shone
Sheer off, disseveral, a star, | death blots black out; nor mark
Is any of him at all so stark
But vastness blurs and | time beats level. Enough! the Resurrection,
A heart's-clarion! A way grief's gasping, | joyless days, dejection.
Across my foundering deck shone
A beacon, an eternal beam. | Flesh fade, and mortal trash
Fall to the residuary worm; | world's wildfire, leave but ash:

In a flash, at a trumpet crash,
I am all at once what Christ is, | since he was what I am, and
This Jack, joke, poor potsherd, | patch, matchwood, immortal
diamond,
Is immortal diamond.

This poem could be a painted canvas – Jack Yeats or Kokoschka, say, but it predates Expressionism. Hopkins wrote it in Co. Dublin in late July 1888, and it has usually been read as a religious poem. Returning to it some years ago, I got interested in the play of wind-driven Irish light as it hits 'roughcast', the 'dazzling whitewash' on the walls of Irish cottages. This light is different from what I saw as the English light of the arched elms' 'shivelights'. This light reminded me of Constable and Paul Nash, while the windy light brought Jack Yeats to mind. I like to see that this was Hopkins's way of imaging the difficult, tense relationship between Ireland and England.

There was a crisis in Anglo-Irish relations in 1886–7, and as his letters to his friend Robert Bridges show, Hopkins responded passionately and sensitively to the strain of the times, and the way they affected him as an English Catholic convert teaching in Dublin's University College. There is a crowded sense of consciousness expanding in the opening lines, and there are deliberate echoes of the civil war in heaven in *Paradise Lost*. Those gangs of roisterers are like the drunken sons of Belial – young cavalier aristocrats – in Milton's epic. The pressure and social edge in Hopkins's lines push what is ostensibly a landscape poem into a hectic apocalyptic vision of the spirit of the age. This is a truly modern, contemporary poem, whose instressed metre has cast the iambic pentameter aside.

More than a year before he wrote it, Hopkins wrote to Bridges:

> Yesterday Archbishop Walsh had a letter in the *Freeman* enclosing a subscription to the defence of Dillon and the other traversers on trial for preaching the Plan of Campaign and saying that the jury was packed and

> a fair trial impossible. The latter was his contribution to the cause of concord and civil order. Today Achbp. Croke has one proposing to pay no taxes. One archbishop backs robbery, the other rebellion; the people in good faith believe and will follow them. You will see, it is the beginning of the end: Home rule or separation is near.

Hopkins is living the social crisis of impending Home Rule or separation, as four months later, in July 1887, he implored Bridges to influence people in England to bring them to 'a just mind and proper resolution about Ireland'. In this letter, he anticipates the stormy, hurrying light of the poem:

> recognise with me that with an unwavering will, or at least a flood of passion on one, the Irish, side and a wavering one or indifference on the other, the English, and the Grand Old Mischiefmaker loose, like the Devil, for a little while and meddling and marring all the fiercer for his hurry, Home Rule is in fact likely to come and even, in spite of the crime, slander, and folly with which its advance is attended, may perhaps in itself be a measure of a sort of equity and, considering that worse might be, of a kind of prudence.

The Grand Old Mischiefmaker is Gladstone, and the imagery of heavenly havoc in the poem echoes Hopkins's view of him as a devilish and impetuous Home Ruler, all wind and wild, hurrying light. Both the poem and the letter rework Milton's Pandemonium, the parliament of fallen angels with its sound of 'blustering winds'. The Heraclitean fire is a metaphor for intense social crisis.

Hopkins detested Gladstone, but he responded keenly to those mass emotions which made Gladstone the great popular leader of the age. The struggling light, the imagery of battle and wrestling are ways of giving imaginative shape to populist politics, to the age of mass demonstrations and 'monster meetings' in Phoenix Park, which Hopkins attended.

Although I was never aware of the homoeroticism in Hopkins's poetry and of his complicated feelings about Whitman's poetry, it wasn't until I read Whitman's 'The Sleepers' that I realised that there is another subject in its opening lines, which is present in Whitman's :

> Well do they do their jobs, those journeymen divine,
> Only from me can they hide nothing and would not if they
> could;
> I reckon I am their boss and they make me a pet besides,
> And surround me and lead me and run ahead when I walk,
> And lift their cunning covers and signify me with stretched
> arms, and resume the way;
> Onward we move, a gay gang of blackguards with
> mirthshouting music and wildflapping pennants of joy.

In adopting Whitman's 'gay gang', Hopkins gives expression to a new political and sexual consciousness that both terrified and attracted him. He would have seen immediately that the phrase is doubly spontaneous and unusual: 'gay' means 'exuberant and spontaneous' (its homosexual significance is more recent), while a 'gang' still carries a colloquial tang which would have appealed to Hopkins: in 'Tom's Garland' he writes of workmen whose 'packs infest the age' – by 'packs' he means rough wolvish gangs.

In the original version of 'The Sleepers', Whitman included a famous sexual passage after the lines:

> Be careful, darkness . . . already, what was it touched me?
> I thought my lover had gone . . . else darkness and he are one.
> I hear the heart-beat . . . I follow . . . I fade away.

This is the culmination of the sweaty lover passage, which was retained, unlike these lines:

> O hotcheeked and blushing! O foolish hectic!
> O for pity's sake, no one must see me now! . . . my clothes
> were stolen while I was abed,
> Now I am thrust forth, where shall I run?

Pier that I saw dimly last night when I looked from the windows.
Pier out from the main, let me catch myself with you and stay ... I will not chafe you;
I feel ashamed to go naked about the world.
And am curious to know where my feet stand ... and what is this flooding me, childhood or manhood ... and the hunger that crosses the bridge between.

The cloth laps a first sweet eating and drinking,
Laps life-swelling yolks ... laps ear of rose-corn, milky and just ripened:
The white teeth stay, and the boss-toothed advances in darkness,
And liquor is spilled on lips and bosoms by touching glasses, and the best liquor afterward.

Whitman's 'the bridge between', Hopkins's 'airy thoroughfare' and the 'broad highway or bridge of chaos', which Satan says makes 'one continent/ Of easy thoroughfare', are melded in Hopkins's risk-taking, allusive imagination. There is a sense of released, joyous, but distrusted sexuality in the opening lines of 'That Nature is a Heraclitean Fire'.

Hopkins begins with a fungus known as the devil's puffball – it is a greyish white and releases black spores when you tread on it. This is his image for storm clouds, and it also carries the Satanic, grand old mischiefmaker Gladstone inside it. The 'torn tufts, tossed pillows' and the verb 'flaunt' all carry sexual connotations, and a reading of 'The Sleepers' reveals that it must have been a crucial poem for Hopkins. With its gashed bodies, its gay gang, its beautiful naked – then beautiful bruised – swimmers, its wrecked ship and prophetic imagery of civil war, it contains several of Hopkins's obsessive subjects.

Hopkins in a letter to Bridges praised what he called the 'savagery' of Whitman's art, and said his rhythm resembled his own in its 'last ruggedness and decomposition' into common prose. The penultimate line of Hopkins's poem literally decomposes, breaks up into hard tactile fragments or potsherds. Hopkins is deliberately smashing the rhythm, packing strongly stressed syllables together in order to enact the break-up of *body/ship/state* so that the 'immortal diamond' of the soul can be made manifest.

Even here, at the very last moment, there is a poignant allusion to Clare's tragic sonnet 'I Am', which begins:

> I am yet what I am none cares or knows,
> I am the self-consumer of my woes.

Hopkins copied Clare's poem into his notebook in his twenties, and it stayed with him, surfacing in 'I am' and 'diamond' at the end of this hugely stretched, unique sonnet, with its far-off prediction of the Easter Rising. Hopkins's 'The Wreck of the Deutschland', which is usually read as a religious poem – and it is one – is also a prediction of the First World War, Europe's first civil war. 'That Nature is a Heraclitean Fire' fuses religion with history and politics, just as Milton does in *Paradise Lost*.

Thomas Given ~ 'A Song for February'

Day in an' day oot on his auld farrant loom,
  Time lengthens the wab o' the past;
Dame Nature steps in like a lamp tae the room,
Hir e'e tae the simmer o' life geein' bloom.
So winter slips by, wi' its mirth an' its gloom,
  As spring is appearin' at last.

The robin gets up an' he lauchs in his glee,
  In view o' the prospect so braw;
Sets his heid tae the side, wi' its feathers agee,
As he spies a bit snaw drop at fit o' the tree,
An' says tae himsel' a'll hae denties tae pree
  By an' by when the splash is awa.

The blackbird keeks oot frae the fog at the broo,
  Gees his neb a bit dicht on a stane;
His eye caught the primrose appearin' in view,
An' the tiny wee violet o' Nature's ain blue;
He sung them a sang o' the auld an' the new –
  A sang we may a' let alane.

The thrush cuff't the leaves 'neath the skep o' the bee,
  An' he tirrl't them aside wae a zest;
I maun hurry awa tae rehearsal, quo he,
This work fits the sparrow far better than me;
His sang pleased the ear frae the tap o' the tree
  As he fell intae tune wae the rest.

Thus Nature provides for hir hoose an' hir wanes,
  An' we may rejoice in the plan;
The wren tae the bluebonnet sings his refrain

On causey o' cottier or lordly domain;
The wagtail looks on withoot shade o' disdain,
May we aye say the same o' the man.

Sometimes we happen on a poem written in dialect. It can seem quaint, local, a change of accent and language, a moment's diversion before we regain the main highway of standard English. In an anthology, it is rather like listening to, say, Tennyson or Hardy do a party piece, and often it was used for comic verse. The Dorset dialect poet William Barnes is different – he influenced Hopkins and Hardy, and is cherished to this day for poems such as 'The Wold Clock', which has an associational and realist aesthetic which Hardy prized. Barnes writes:

Who now do wind his chaïn, a-twin'd
As he do run his hours,
Or meäke a gloss to sheen across
His door, wi' golden flow'rs,
Since he've a-sounded out the last
Still hours our dear good mother passed?

And Hardy echoes him, as he observes 'shiny familiar' old furniture:

Hands behind hands, growing paler and paler,
As in a mirror a candle-flame
Shows images of itself, each frailer
As it recedes, though the eye may frame
Its shape the same.

Barnes is a one-off, a quoof. But Thomas Given, from a village in Co. Antrim called Cullybackey, a name always pronounced with a triumphant yelp on the last two syllables – 'Cully*backey*!' – is part of a community of what were known as weaver poets. These poets belonged to the Ulster Enlightenment, wrote in the Burns stanza and espoused the Rights of Man. Some, like Thomas Given (1850–1917) who worked on the family farm, were freemasons, convivial men who liked to address each other in verse letters and move between Ulster Scots and standard poetic diction.

We can see this in the Co. Down weaver poet Hugh Porter, who in a verse epistle 'To the Reverend TT' mentions an anthology called *Elegant Extracts in Poetry Selected for the Improvement of Young Persons:*

> Among the rest that me attracts
> There's one of which I hear great cracks
> An' that's the *Elegant Extracts.*
> So if ye hae it,
> Your humble rhymer Sir, expects
> Or hopes ye'll gi'e it.

Making play with the rather pretentious title of the anthology, Porter employs the vocal, convivial phrase 'great cracks' to inflect *Extracts* with a witty accent, and claim it as native – *Extracks*. This in turn makes 'your humble rhymer Sir' egalitarian – mock formal – in the best Burnsian manner. These poets know how to move in and out of a douce, polite voice and when to assume a tender, intimate voice which, as I say, is convivial.

In 'A Song for February', Thomas Given takes Standard Habbie – the Burns stanza used by Hugh Porter – and puts the first AAA rhymes after the second line just as the penultimate line in Standard Habbie does, while Given's second and penultimate lines mirror the fourth and last line in Standard Habbie. But where that form uses four iambic feet, Given uses eleven syllables in his first line and rejects the iambic pentameter:

> Day in/ and day oot/ on his auld/ farrant/ loom

The adjective 'auld' is communal – as in 'auld lang syne' – and 'farrant' means 'travelling'. But the dialect or vernacular voice isn't simply a matter of translating one word into another – it is rapid and concise, saying 'at fit' not 'at the foot'. Similarly 'wi'its' elides 'with its' and 'o' the tree' 'of the tree'. There is something in this voice which likes the irreducible fact of 'it' and 'its' – a common playground term of derision is to shout 'Look at IT!' This can be felt in the internal rhyme in 'a bit snowdrop at fit o' the tree', which places and roots the perception. There is a similar sly joke later, when Nature provides for 'hir hoose an' hir wanes' (children). But the best lines are:

> The blackbird keeks oot frae the fog at the broo,
> Gees his neb a bit dicht on a stane.

Commenting on these lines, the Northern Irish poet John Hewitt says:

> *To keek* means something more precise than simply 'to look, 'to peep'. There is always a furtiveness about it. With *oot frae* there should be no trouble. *The fog at the broo* means roughly 'the long grass left standing after winter' in the ditch at the side of the field. For the second line, *Gees his neb* is fairly obviously 'Gives his beak'. *A bit dicht on a stane: dicht*, Robert Burns used to spell this word *dight*, means something more exact than 'to wipe'; it means rather a quick flick-of-a-wipe. My mother always spoke of giving her nose a dicht of powder – *a bit dicht* makes the flick even lighter. There aren't three words in English which could catch that gesture. You couldn't offer word for word translation.

That phrase 'bit dicht' – the tough practical *it* in both words – has the spondaic definition which is there in the opening line: 'Day in an' day oot'.

As Hewitt shows in his glossary to his anthology *The Rhyming Weavers*, the word 'broo' means 'the higher side of a ditch', so the line is highly concentrated. The blackbird's quick 'flick-of-a-wipe' is an image for the poet's verbal dexterity, the vernacular confidence in sentence-sound which he feels. His song of the 'auld an' the new' hints at a political theme, which he brushes away in the last line of the stanza, only to return to it in the last lines where the cottier's paved yard and the lord's demesne are given equal treatment by the wren, supported by the unsnobbish bluebonnet.

The political theme is present in Samuel Thompson's 'To a Hedgehog', which was published just after the 1798 Uprising:

> Gudefaith thou disna want for pikes
>   Baith sharp and rauckle;
> Thou looks (Lord save's) array'd in spikes
>   A creepin' heckle.

A 'heckle' is a board with spikes for dressing flax, while 'rauckle' means 'strong' – both words are more than shaggy, they are prickly and abrasive. Such words demonstrate that these weaver poets enjoyed and insisted on using an at times abrasive language, which reflected the hard work and the implements they were habituated to. Dante characterised such dialect words as 'yrsuta', 'shaggy', and drew on them as he shaped Italian regional dialects into a national language. This national ambition is subtly present in 'A Song for February' where the rhyme *man/plan* gestures at 'A Man's a Man for all that', at the Rights of Man, and a more egalitarian political plan or design.

Reading a single poem by a weaver poet, we realise that we cannot isolate it from its language, culture and locality – we need to read it communally, as part of a group whose base is its first audience of fellow poets. We need, therefore, to read it through John Hewitt's anthology *The Rhyming Weavers*, where we will find this stanza from Robert Huddleston's 'The Cobbler':

> There sits a tinker wi' his tins,
>   A turner wi' his ladles,
> A gleg tongu'd spunkie's cryin' spoons,
>   Anither's at her fables.

That adjective 'gleg' means 'sharp, keen, quick-witted, fluent in speech', and comes from the Old Norse *glegger*, which means 'sharp-sighted, clever'. The word 'spunkie', from the Scottish Gaelic *spong*, earlier *sponc*, 'tinder', is a noun meaning, I would guess, 'an energetic character'. Street cries, the jossing badinage between tradesmen and buyers in markets, are part of the spunky life of the vernacular, and it is that sprung rhythm these poets celebrate. Seamus Heaney's *Wintering Out* (1973) draws on their lithe, natural language and their cadences. In 'To George Seferis in the Underworld', Heaney refers to the dialect word 'seggan', which is given to various pieces of reeds, rushes and sedges, and calls it:

> a dialect blade, hoar and harder
> than what it has turned into
> these latter days:
> sedge, marshmallow, rubber-dagger stuff.

Here, he is summoning poets like Thomas Given and Robert Huddleston, as well as John Clare and Thomas Hardy, and reminding us that writing is a social act, not simply a private commitment. These poets don't simply look out, they kick out.

Robert Frost ~ 'The Investment'

Over back where they speak of life as staying
(You couldn't call it living, for it ain't),
There was an old, old house renewed with paint,
And in it a piano loudly playing.

Out in the plowed ground in the cold a digger,
Among unearthed potatoes standing still,
Was counting winter dinners, one a hill,
With half an ear to the piano's vigor.

All that piano and new paint back there,
Was it some money suddenly come into?
Or some extravagance young love had been to?
Or old love on an impulse not to care –

Not to sink under being man and wife,
But get some color and music out of life?

The title has the first *ih* sound, which will accrue weight later. The word 'it' takes slight stress through the repetition.

The two opening lines have what Frost calls sentence sound:

> A sentence is a sound itself on which other sounds called words may be strung . . .
>
> A Patch of Old Snow
> In the corner of the wall where the bushes haven't been trimmed, there is a patch of old snow like a blow-away newspaper that has come to rest there. And it is dirty as with the print and news of a day I have forgotten, if I ever read it.
>
> Now that is good except for what I may call certain points of recognition in it: patch of old snow in a corner of the wall, – you know what that

is. You know what a blowaway newspaper is. You know the curious dirt on old snow and last of all you know how easily you forget what you read in papers.

Now for the sentence sounds. We will look for the marked ones because they are easiest to discuss. The first sentence will do but it is merely ordinary and bookish: it is entirely subordinate in interest to the meaning of the words strung on it. But half the effectiveness of the second sentence is in the very special tone with which you must say news of a day I have forgotten – if I ever read it. You must be able to say, Oh yes one knows how that goes. (There is some adjective to describe the intonation or cadence, but I won't hunt for it.)

One of the least successful of the poems in my book is almost saved by a final striking sentence-sound ('Asking for Roses'):

Not caring very much *what* she supposes.

Take my 'November Guest'. Did you know at once how we say such sentences as these when we talk?

She thinks I have no eye for these.
Not yesterday I learned etc.
But it were vain to tell her so.

Get away from the sing-song. You must hear and recognise in the last line the sentence sound that supports, No use in telling him so.

And Frost then gives a series of examples:

My father used to say
You're a liar!
If a hen and a half lay an egg and a half etc
A long long time ago –
Put it there old man (Offering your hand)
I aint a going to hurt you, so you neednt be scared.
...

It is so and not otherwise that we get the variety that makes it fun to write and read. *The ear does it.* The ear is the only true writer and the only true reader. I have known people who could read without hearing the sentence sounds and they were the fastest readers. Eye readers we call them. They can get the meaning by glances. But they are bad readers because they miss the best part of what a good writer puts into his work.

> Remember that the sentence sound often says more than the words. It may even as in irony convey a meaning opposite to the words.

Frost is arguing for vernacular poetry and it is important to remember that not all poetry is vernacular – Spenser, Milton, Keats, Tennyson aren't.

The third line of 'The Investment' shifts the iambic pattern:

> There was an old, old house renewed with paint

The line has six stresses because 'old house' is a spondee. This slows the line, something which also happens in the second line with the internal rhyme *living/staying*, an effect which lengthens the caesura.

The alliteration on *p* gives 'piano' prominence. Line 4 scans:

> And in it a piano loudly playing

The trisyllabic 'piano' moves speedily but there is then a substantial caesural pause, which isolates the trochaic 'loudly playing'. In anticipation – a type of metrical prolepsis – 'loudly' is slightly isolated because it rhymes internally with 'plowed'.

Frost begins the second quatrain with a preposition, just as he began the first line with a treble preposition. 'Over back there' is reminiscent of the opening of 'Directive':

> Back out of all this now too much for us,
> Back in a time made simple by the loss.

Noticing that 'plowed' and 'loudly' rhyme, we can note that 'old, old' and 'piano' rhyme – the effect isolates 'piano', which also, because it is unexpected, breaks free from that double 'old'. The run of *d* sounds – *old old plowed ground cold digger* – also impact on 'loudly'. Again 'plowed ground' is slightly stilled by the triangulating internal rhyme.

Frost varies what used to be called masculine and feminine rhymes in each quatrain; *into/been (bin) to* is a full rhyme. The plosive *p* from 'paint' passes to *piano plowed potatoes,* but the last two can't hold onto it because it is reasserted by the repeated *piano piano* and *paint*. There is also an internal rhyme on 'piano' and 'potatoes', which is extended by 'piano's'. That *ih* sound we first meet in the title gathers momentum – *in in digger still winter dinners hill* – to reverberate in 'vigor'. There is strength and trueness in the *vigor/digger* rhyme because the *g* in 'digger' chimes with the *g* that begins 'ground'.

There is a sight internal rhyme on 'unearthed' and 'ear', which makes the contrast between earthy digger and the piano's vigour marked. The *uh* sounds in *some money suddenly* and *some* impact on 'young love'. The *v* in 'love' heightens retrospectively the *v* in 'extravagance', which as it is the only word in the poem of four syllables stands out. The first *a* in that word also stands out as it echoes the *a* in 'piano' while the *p* in 'piano' touches on 'impulse'. The final couplet with its married masculine rhyme is textured by the guttural *g* and *ks*. The result is one of Frost's most accomplished poems, but one which tends to be ignored by critics.

Robert Frost ~ from 'A Servant to Servants'

I didn't make you know how glad I was
To have you come and camp here on our land.
I promised myself to get down some day
And see the way you lived, but I don't know!
With a houseful of hungry men to feed
I guess you'd find. . . . It seems to me
I can't express my feelings any more
Than I can raise my voice or want to lift
My hand (oh, I can lift it when I have to).
Did ever you feel so? I hope you never.
It's got so I don't even know for sure
Whether I *am* glad, sorry, or anything.
There's nothing but a voice-like left inside
That seems to tell me how I ought to feel,
And would feel if I wasn't all gone wrong.
You take the lake. I look and look at it.
I see it's a fair, pretty sheet of water.
I stand and make myself repeat out loud
The advantages it has, so long and narrow,
Like a deep piece of some old running river
Cut short off at both ends. It lies five miles
Straight away through the mountain notch
From the sink window where I wash the plates,
And all our storms come up toward the house,
Drawing the slow waves whiter and whiter and whiter.
It took my mind off doughnuts and soda biscuit
To step outdoors and take the water dazzle
A sunny morning, or take the rising wind
About my face and body and through my wrapper,

When a storm threatened from the Dragon's Den,
And a cold chill shivered across the lake.
I see it's a fair pretty sheet of water,
Our Willoughby! How did you hear of it?
I expect, though, everyone's heard of it.
In a book about ferns? Listen to that!
You let things more like feathers regulate
Your going and coming. And you like it here?
I can see how you might. But I don't know!
It would be different if more people came,
For then there would be business. As it is,
The cottages Len built, sometimes we rent them,
Sometimes we don't.

This is the beginning of a long monologue spoken by a farmer's wife to an itinerant camped on her land. She is lonely and overworked, stuck in a household of men, and worried she may go mad, as her uncle did – he was kept in a cage in an upstairs room in the family farmhouse. Frost catches the cadences of her thoughts, the 'voice-like left inside'. As she talks the lake grows in significance: at first it seems female, 'a fair, pretty sheet of water', perhaps an image of herself as a young girl or bride? Perhaps a hint for him to tell her she is still pretty? It could be a virginal image, an unstained bedsheet, though a sheet can also be a screen, a shroud. It is lengthened by the long *ee* in 'repeat' in the next line, which momentarily halts its forward movement. We speak of someone being as white as a sheet, and also we write on sheets of paper. Maybe Frost is figuring one of his poems, written or printed on a sheet of paper, like 'a deep piece of some old running river'. A river that runs underground, emerging only briefly into the daylight? The sunny lake appears innocent while the old running river is the opposite, except both are deep, part of the same apparent but illusory continuum.

This non-existent river is 'cut short off at both ends'. This is a disturbing image, a phallic image on one level, on another an image of futurelessness and lack of children. The lake begins at the 'sink window', where she washes the plates, so that the *lake/river/sink* image is also womb-like, but the site of unproductive domestic drudgery. Her sense of imprisonment prepares us for the moment later in the poem where she describes how her mother 'had to lie and hear love things made dreadful' by her husband's mad brother shouting in the night. He would pull the wooden bars of his cage until they twanged 'like bow and bowstring'. Then she clinches this by adding: 'His hands had worn them smooth as any oxbow'. She means a wooden collar for an ox, so this doubles the imprisonment motif.

Wood is in Frost's imagination when he has her refer to the cleft in the mountain as a 'notch'. On the one hand, Frost liked to compare poems to crafted wood, axe handles for example. A notch is cut with a knife – again a threatening phallic image (she is trapped in a wholly masculine world), but the effect is vaginal, though dry and negative (the word contains 'not', which we can also read as 'knot', representing marriage, as well as a hard, stubborn fault in a plank of wood). Crusoe says: 'Upon the sides of this square post I cut every day a notch with my knife', and traditionally we record days and victories with notches. This mountain notch has a stuck, trapped, unbudging quality. That *tch* sound reverberates rather like the wooden bars of the mad uncle's cage twanging like a bow and bowstring. Come to think of it, an arrow – love's symbol – has a notch at one end. There is also something snug about the word – it is close to 'niche'. Frost, who was a gifted classical scholar, may have known it came, via the old French *oche*, 'notch', from the Latin *obecare*, 'to cut off'. We return, here, to the apparent river 'cut off at both ends'. However, the *OED* gives a third definition: 'US. a narrow opening or defile through mountains, a deep narrow pass.' This has to be the primary meaning.

There is a lyric, intense moment when she describes how the

storms draw 'The slow waves whiter and whiter and whiter'. There may be a bridal whiteness in this image, which is climatic and idealistic. The repeated *l* sounds make a soothing contrast to the pinched *ih* sounds in 'It' and 'sink'. Also 'whiter' repeats 'miles' and 'I' to represent almost a visionary freedom.

In the next line 'doughnuts and soda' are given emphasis because they pick up 'slow' in the previous line. In another poem, 'Directive', Frost describes visiting a deserted village, and then directs us to weep

> For a house that is no more a home,
> But only a belilaced cellar hole,
> Now slowly closing like a dent in dough.

Frost plays subtle changes on the many *o*s in 'Directive' – it is both everything and nothing. Here, it is vaginal, responding to a phallic thumb. In 'A Servant to Servants' the doughnuts – 'gravy rings' in the North of Ireland – are also vaginal, but the soda biscuits' are triply dry, soda being alkaline, sodium carbonate, a chemical. An association with washing soda starts up 'whiter' – more drudgery. The two *ih* sounds in 'biscuit' are limiting, narrow, after the long *o* in 'soda'.

Her sexual responsiveness follows: twice she uses 'take' in the next line –'take the water dazzle . . . take the rising wind'. Soda, we remember, is a rising agent, but the wind is also sexual, yet spiritual as it penetrates her wrapper and makes her look briefly pregnant. She is attracted to the man camping on their land.

The ominous Dragon's Den and 'a cold chill shivered' play against this erotic moment – these two *ih* sounds pitch in hard. But she turns them round – or tries to – by saying: 'I see it's a fair, pretty sheet of water,/ Our Willoughby!' We are in the bedroom here, but 'pretty' is made uncomfortable by the memory it carries of 'chill' and 'shivered'. It's a phrase she likes to repeat, a phrase that is both uplifting and inert, a cliché. The *d*s in 'doughnuts' and 'soda' impact on 'dazzle' and 'outdoors' to give them strong prominence. But the *d*s culminate in 'Dragon's Den' and seem to enclose her.

Frost's choice of 'Willoughby' for the lake is complex – the *ih* is back in place but so is the *o*. In Shakespeare's sonnets 'will' is his first name and his phallus. I see 'lough' and 'willow' in the name Willoughby – Ophelia's body is found by a willow on the river bank, and willows traditionally weep. The willow is female and if we add in 'be' this becomes an ontological image of dwelling in a particular place. The name Willoughby, which she personalises with the familiar 'our', as if it's a child – and she has no children – also has 'lough' locked in it, so we're back with the lake; or rather, the word fits the lake exactly. The book about ferns brings pubic hair somewhere into the image, while the Anglo-Norman name has a faintly aristocratic timbre. On the other hand, Frost said that we can't count every possible meaning of a word, just as we always comb our hair in the one direction. On the other hand again – and he didn't say this – we sometimes tousle our hair slightly so it doesn't look too neat, too *en brosse*.

The man she addresses she wants to stay with her, as she imagines and rejects living in a tent with him and those he shares a tent with. She is lonely, frustrated, overworked, desperate to talk, but somehow, despite the general critical view of her, not convincingly mentally ill.

Isaac Rosenberg ~ 'Break of Day in the Trenches'

The darkness crumbles away.
It is the same old Druid Time as ever.
Only a live thing leaps my hand,
A queer sardonic rat,
As I pull the parapet's poppy
To stick behind my ear.
Droll rat, they would shoot you if they knew
Your cosmopolitan sympathies.
Now you have touched this English hand
You will do the same to a German
Soon, no doubt, if it be your pleasure
To cross the sleeping green between.
It seems, odd thing, you grin as you pass
Strong eyes, fine limbs, haughty athletes,
Less chanced than you for life,
Bonds to the whims of murder,
Sprawled in the bowels of the earth,
The torn fields of France.
What do you see in our eyes
At the shrieking iron and flame
Hurl'd through still heavens?
What quaver – what heart aghast?
Poppies whose roots are in man's veins
Drop, and are ever dropping,
But mine in my ear is safe –
Just a little white with the dust.

In 1886 Dovber Rosenberg, Isaac's father, who was a native of Lithuania, was ordered to report as a conscript in the Russian army. He was a Tolstoyan and a student of the Torah, and military service was against his moral principles. He crossed the border into Germany and at Hamburg boarded a ship which he believed was bound for the United States. The boat docked at Hull; Dovber disembarked and caught a train to Leeds, then moved to Bristol. He sent for his wife and daughter. Isaac was born on 25 November 1890, and seven years later the family moved to the East End of London. Rosenberg attended the Slade, a member of a generation of famous artists that included David Bomberg, Mark Gertler and Stanley Spencer. He enlisted in 1915, and told Edward Marsh, 'I never joined the army for patriotic reasons. Nothing can justify war. I suppose we must all fight to get the trouble over.'

In this, his most famous and assured poem, he watches dawn breaking. If his father had caught a different boat, he might not be here at the front. His first line draws on an early untitled poem which begins:

> The world rumbles by me – can I heed?
> The rose it is crimson – and I bleed.

This couplet draws on Yeats's early nationalist poems, where red roses symbolise Ireland. Rosenberg began a later poem, 'At Sea-Point', set in a costal town in South Africa, like this:

> Let the earth crumble away,
> The heavens fade like a breath,
> The sea go up in a cloud,
> And its hills be given to death.

This means that 'crumble' has inside it the word 'rumbles', and when Rosenberg uses 'crumbles' in the first line of 'Break of Day in the Trenches' he wants us to hear the rumble of an imminent barrage. And it has bleeding roses and an earth-crumbling apocalypse inside it too. The emphasis falls on the unexpected phrase 'Druid Time', which with its initial capitals stands out like a monument, perhaps like Stonehenge.

Rosenberg justified the second line in a letter to Edward Marsh (4 August 1916) which he sent with a fair copy of the poem:

> I am enclosing a poem which I wrote in the trenches, which is surely as simple as ordinary talk. You might object to the second line as a bit vague, but that was the best way I could express the sanctity of dawn.

This may be Rosenberg pretending a sanctity he doesn't express in the opening lines of the poem, but which is there in the cosmopolitan rat at the end. Siegfried Sassoon did not detect that quality, saying that the poem had for him 'a poignant and nostalgic quality. Sensuous front-line existence is there, hateful and repellent, unforgettable and inescapable.'

The word 'Druid' carries overtones of blood sacrifice, which are there in the bleeding roses of the early poem. Earlier that year, Irish nationalist revolutionaries led by Patrick Pearse had offered themselves in blood sacrifice in the Easter Rising. The crucifixion is present in the pagan adjective Rosenberg has chosen, and as a Jew he must feel uneasy about this and about the English ethnic nationalism which sometimes uses Stonehenge as its symbol. A few months earlier, he had written a short poem, 'The Jew':

> The blonde, the bronze, the ruddy,
> With the same heaving blood,
> Keep tide to the moon of Moses.
> Then why do they sneer at me?

In a letter, he said of joining the 12th Suffolk Regiment, 'my being a Jew makes it bad among these wretches'. In this poem, he takes that anti-Semitic symbol, the rat, used by T. S. Eliot and discussed by Anthony Julius in his study of Eliot's anti-Semitism, and turns it tenderly into a real rat that is also 'cosmopolitan', like a Jewish or other intellectual, who is sceptical of patriotism and simple national identity (Eamon De Valera criticised what he regarded as the rootless cosmopolitanism of Joyce's *Ulysses*).

In the second line, the long first syllable *droo* in 'Druid' lengthens the word, but the short second syllable *id* moves it on briskly, because this is the third *ih* sound and we've already heard two *d* sounds. Also the three strong stresses on 'same old Druid' emphasise the sameyness of another dawn in wartime. The long *i* in 'time' slows the line again and the *t* takes stress from 'It', starting the line again, ever so slightly. The extra unstressed, eleventh syllable also protracts the line. This line is also stretched because 'as ever' and 'the same' are almost identical. The line is beautifully spontaneous, flatly spoken, as Rosenberg intended. We seem to hear his speaking voice, as we do in that tender last line, where the *it* in 'little' brings the first word of the poem back into play, but bitter now, tiny, harder.

Behind 'Druid', I think, lies a now-forgotten epic poem, which was much admired by Edward Thomas – Charles M. Doughty's *The Dawn in Britain*, which was published in 1906, just ten years before. There are many druids in Doughty's poem, and early in the first volume this dawn passage occurs:

> That druid went forth; and when he came again,
> Bright messenger of sacred dawn, is risen,
> The morning star. Then to the Briton sire,
> He spoke, how severally the bowels renounce,
> Propitious is the mind of Gaul's great gods.
> On turven altars, dight the victims' flesh;
> Then, suddenly, a three-forked flame of lightning smote,
> Which everyone consumed, to the green sods.

Druids and human sacrifice go together, which means that Rosenberg and his fellow soldiers and the enemy they face are future victims of history or 'old Druid Time'. Doughty calls dawn 'sacred' and so does Rosenberg in his letter, but 'the same old' is wearily secular.

We hear *dread* and *dead* in Druid and *rue* (*id* is pushing it). With its initial and final dentals, the word is heavy, like a lid, or a slab on a sarcophagus.

There's a lift in the *i* sound in 'Time', which flicks over to 'live', like a leaping spark, and emphasises the rat's motion. Repeated in 'I', it also emphasises the sudden action of his hand pulling the poppy. The gutturals in *queer sardonic stick* tell a different story: these rough *k*s are stuck, the last two of them, to the *ih* sound which is strong in the second line. However, the *o* in 'sardonic' is picked up by 'poppy', whose plosives are already emphasised by 'parapet'. Again, the *p* in 'cosmopolitan' picks up on this, and the third *o* is also emphasised so that *pol* stands out starkly, as if it's a word on its own. This isolated sound gives force and authority to the only five-syllabled word in the poem.

The three *ee* sounds in 'sleeping green between' make the middle word uneasy. Rosenberg admired Blake, and I detect the end of the sinister nurse's song – 'And sport no more seen/ On the darkening green' – in this strange transposition of a village green to no man's land. It's a queasy moment.

There may be a glance at Rupert Brooke's '1914' in 'fine limbs, haughty athletes'. Brooke's sonnet sequence celebrates the outbreak of the war (it contains his most famous poem, 'The Soldier'), and in the first sonnet, 'Peace', he speaks of 'our youth' turning 'as swimmers into cleanness leaping/ Glad from a world grown old and cold and weary'. Rosenberg knows there's no way he can repudiate and transcend the world's old Druid time.

The internal rhymes in *limbs/whims* and *chanced/France* colour the words, while 'Sprawled' and 'bowels' assonate. The word 'bowels' was traditionally used to signify compassion, so a feeling for what has also been done to the earth is present here and in 'torn'.

The word 'still' takes on an extra weight because it picks up the two preceding *l*s in 'flame' and 'hurl'd'. Noticing the proximity of 'flame' and 'still', I recall Yeats's 'The Valley of the Black Pig':

We who still labour by the cromlech on the shore,
The grey cairn on the hill, when day sinks drowned in dew,
Being weary of the world's empires, bow down to you,
Master of the still stars and of the flaming door.

The repeated *st* cadence is steely, and the last line communicates a fascination with heroic combat that is entirely missing from Rosenberg's front-line lyric.

A devoted scholar has suggested that Rosenberg is thinking of Blake's 'The Tyger':

And what shoulder, and what art,
Could twist the sinews of thy heart?
And when the heart began to beat,
What dread hand and what dread feet?

What the lever? What the chain?
In what furnace was thy brain?
What the anvil? What dread grasp
Dare its deadly terrors clasp?

Against the thunder and flame of the heavenly blacksmith, Rosenberg sets the ephemerality of the poppy, whose *pop* at the beginning of the last four lines is a tiny explosion picked up by 'drop' and 'dropping' to emphasise the flower's vulnerability – it drops as blood drops. Rosenberg's painter's eye is matching poppy, blood, the redness of dawn – he refuses to offer a variation on the heroic, Homeric rosy-fingered dawn.

Rosenberg's lovely last line is as simple as ordinary talk: it is braced by four *ts*, softened by *th*, has a tiny pause after 'little' and a slightly longer spoken pause after 'white', before the final anapaest lilts out of the previous iambic feet ('Jūst ă' is a reversed iambic foot). The last word 'dust' takes a shade more stress because it carries 'Just', and this adds the dust of death to the actual dust on the poppy. The slight paleness hints at fear, even the possibility of surrender, but not really because it is only a little white. That word 'little', as I said, picks up 'It' at the beginning of the second line, and brings the absolute fact of a new day, new light, into the image. It is a tender and loving diminutive, the equivalent of 'wee bit', as Rosenberg's painter's eye brings the crumbling darkness-and-light into the specks of white dust on the red poppy.

Rosenberg's poem was published in the famous Chicago magazine *Poetry* in December 1916. He was killed in action at Arras on 1 April 1917. His body was one of six that could not be individually named. These six soldiers are buried at St Laurence-Blagny, near Arras. Each soldier has an individual gravestone. Beneath Rosenberg's name, dates and regimental details are the Star of David and the words 'Artist and Poet'.

Edward Thomas ~ 'The Owl'

Downhill I came, hungry, and yet not starved;
Cold, yet had heat within me that was proof
Against the North wind; tired, yet so that rest
Had seemed the sweetest thing under a roof.

Then at the inn I had food, fire, and rest,
Knowing how hungry, cold, and tired was I.
All of the night was quite barred out except
An owl's cry, a most melancholy cry

Shaken out long and clear upon the hill,
No merry note, nor cause of merriment.
But one telling me plain what I escaped
And others could not, that night, as in I went.

And salted was my food, and my repose,
Salted and sobered, too, by the bird's voice
Speaking for all who lay under the stars,
Soldiers and poor, unable to rejoice.

The spondees at the start and the end of the first line – 'Dōwnhīll', 'nōt stārved' – create a heavy-booted marching quality. They wear army boots and give the line weight and momentum, but that momentum pushes the line downhill, a word that always signifies failure: when things, a business, say, start to go downhill they are doomed. If the inn were at the top of the hill, it would signify success and freedom. We achieve something when we reach the top of a hill, but here that initial *d* is releasing anxieties, which are emphasised by the final *d* in 'starved'. That word is used in Ireland, where 'starved with the cold' means not 'hungry', but 'dead', from the German *sterben*. This leads me back to the 'hun' in 'hungry'. The war, which was to kill Edward Thomas in the Battle of Arras in 1917, is inside everything he thinks and feels. Those *d*s in 'Downhill', 'starved' and 'cold' figure death, and they continue in 'wind', 'tired' and 'seemed'. These are the subliminal flickers, the tiny signals, which the opening line sends out: it means, after all, something more than 'I walked downhill, I was hungry but not starving.' There is something biblical in that cadence 'and yet not starved', which might explain why the line is both simple and momentous. Its force suggests a cross-country march.

The heat within him is like proofed spirit, protection, armour, against the north wind, blowing from a place of danger – North Germany, Russia. The north in Milton is always barbarous and satanic, and Thomas, like Milton, keeps to the southern counties and Wales. Here, he writes mainly in the persona of a literary pilgrim, like Hazlitt or Wordsworth, both of whom he celebrates in his topographical study, *A Literary Pilgrim*.

For Hazlitt, in his essays, the arrival at an inn is always a crucial and enhancing moment, but the wandering freedom of the essay mode is here constrained to a marching rhythm, so that there is something tight and compressed about it. The opening guttural in 'Cold' is a sound that carries the initial guttural in 'came' and the guttural in 'hungry'. The word 'proof' has its rhyme word 'roof' in it, so there is comfort and security doubly inside it.

Then he uses 'yet' again. This reminds us of 'and yet', which had opened a train of possibility, not-yet-ness, the about to happen, which is death. Here, 'food, fire and rest' suggests comfort, peaceful sleep, but that word at the end of the line is a version of 'requiescat', a verb which is often accompanied by 'in pace'. The *o* in 'so' drops down the *o* in 'cold', making that tiny word almost shiver, and passes it on to 'repose'. Then the internal rhyme in 'seemed the sweetest', with *th* picked up by 'thing', creates a comforting harmony under 'a roof'. At the start of the next stanza he reaches that roof whose *r* and *f* are replicated in 'food, fire and rest', as well as in the internal rhyme *roof/food*. The long *oo* sound, initiated by 'proof', is picked up by 'food' in the first line of the last stanza, and in 'poor' in the last line. It is the sound of the owl's *toowit-toowhoo*, subtly infiltrating the poem, instead of being mimicked in it.

The first line of the second stanza contains a triplet of nouns, then in the next line there is an adjectival triplet – the danger here is that this is becoming a tic, which will undermine the poem. He therefore wipes out this danger with the next line: 'All of the night was quite barred out except'. This suggests that the darkness is shut out and that all within is warmth and light. But he has introduced 'night' into the line, so it's present, while 'barred' brings prison bars to mind, with the night behind them – he is trapped, as the internal rhyme *night/quite* demonstrates. There is an ambiguity in 'quite': the night is either absolutely or almost barred out, but mentioning night, as I said, brings it squarely into the picture .

The look of this poem is four square and traditional, like, we assume, the inn. The four quatrains rhyme ABCB, but the A rhymes are either faint or non-existent, which introduces an uncertainty that is part of the ground of anxiety in the poem. The owl's cry is a downhill moment, but it is shaken out 'loud and clear,' like a signal, a message, a statement, which dominates the hill. Here, doom speaks its long *oo*s.

As has often been pointed out, that phrase 'merry note' comes from Shakespeare's *Love's Labours Lost*:

> When icicles hang by the wall
>   And Dick the shepherd blows his nail,
> And Tom bears logs into the hall,
>   And milk comes frozen home in pail;
> When blood is nipt, and ways be foul,
> Then nightly sings the staring owl

Tu-whoo!
To-whit, Tu-whoo! A merry note!
While greasy Joan doth keel the pot.

Thomas cancels that old English, as Shakespeare and Hazlitt call it, merriness, but at the same time he gives it room outside the inn. Hazlitt has an essay, 'Merry England', in which he celebrates English rural games and pursuits – Thomas wants that merriness recalled as loss. The darkness of war threatens it.

The owl's cry is a version of plain speaking – traditionally English, even Hazlittian – but that word 'plain' in the middle of the sentence carries 'pain' inside it. The verb 'escaped' reminds us of the prison effect, the claustrophobia, of the second stanza. This is recapitulated in the tiny subordinated clause 'that night', which compresses everything in the poem before it. The dentals in 'that night' are repeated in 'salted' – the cadence here is that of the Authorised Version of the Bible.

The word 'stars' takes us back to 'starved', and the image here is of a battlefield, where there is no possibility of victory. Most famously, Margaret Thatcher is remembered to have used 'rejoice' of the British victory in the Falklands (actually she was referring to the bloodless victory on the island of South Georgia). Later, Tony Blair said, cunningly, that he was trying not to say 'rejoice' over Iraq. The word 'lay' suggests both sleep – or trying to sleep – and death. That word 'unable' in the middle of the last line takes us back to the middle of the first line – 'hungry' – so that we are back with the Hun, a word Thomas would have left to Kipling, but which he wanted to infiltrate his poem, like that painful *oo* sound.

Thomas Hardy ~ 'In Time of "The Breaking of Nations"' and 'The Self-Unseeing'

I

Only a man harrowing clods
In a slow silent walk
With an old horse that stumbles and nods
Half asleep as they stalk.

II

Only thin smoke without flame
From the heaps of couch-grass;
Yet this will go onward the same
Though Dynasties pass.

III

Yonder a maid and her wight
Come whispering by:
War's annals will cloud into night
Ere their story die.

~

Here is the ancient floor,
Footworn and hollowed and thin,
Here was the former door
Where the dead feet walked in.

She sat here in her chair,
Smiling into the fire;
He who played stood there
Bowing it higher and higher.

Childlike, I danced in a dream;
Blessings emblazoned that day;
Everything glowed with a gleam;
Yet we were looking away!

'In Time of "The Breaking of Nations"' seems to report an everyday observation, but its sources go much deeper. In his disguised autobiography, Hardy says that on the day 'the bloody battle' of Gravelotte was fought he and his future wife, Emma Lavinia Gifford, were reading Tennyson in the grounds of her brother's rectory in Cornwall:

> It was at this time and spot that Hardy was struck by the incident of the old horse harrowing the arable field in the valley below, which, when in far later years it was recalled to him by a still bloodier war, he made it into a little poem.

Asked for a war poem for the *Saturday Review* in December 1915, he remembered the incident and wrote the poem.

This tiny lyric, with its three numbered stanzas, is commemorative, not simply placed in the apparently peaceful present. Those Latin numerals are quietly and unobtrusively monumental, and they are amplified by the two, slightly jarring Latinate words 'Dynasties' and 'annals'. The verb 'harrowing' literally describes the act of ploughing a field, but we remember its use as a metaphor describing a painful experience, and we perhaps recall medieval images of Christ's harrowing of hell. It derives from an Old English verb, *hargian*, which in the thirteenth century became 'to harry' – there is battle in that word, so the plough is remotely a type of weapon: 'harrowing' is not an irenic verb.

The *o* in 'harrowing' is repeated in 'slow' and 'old', which creates a recalcitrant, dragging effect. The *d* in 'clods' establishes dominance from the beginning – we catch its hard dental in *nods onward Dynasties yonder maid cloud*, and in the very last word *die*. The sleepy movement of the ploughman and his old, weary horse has a deathly determinism – ordinary life may be going on, but the war's determinism has infected movement, making it slow and painful. Any optimism we may draw from the apparently timeless image carries its denial.

A ploughed field can resemble a battlefield over which soldiers stumble – Hardy gives no place name, so perhaps this is No Man's Land? That verb 'stalk' is sinister – we stalk prey. The *walk/stalk* rhyme denies the leisureliness of walking: both horse and ploughman move like automatons, like figures in Hardy's deterministic epic of the Napoleonic wars, *The Dynasts*.

The thin, flameless smoke is unsettling too – we recall the adage 'no smoke without fire', and recognise that this undisturbed landscape is somehow unreal. It doesn't add up. The heaps of couch-grass could be bodies, chucked aside like weeds. A couch is a piece of furniture – the monumental again, if we remember the couch and shrouded corpse in the illustration Hardy did for 'Thoughts of Phena' in *Wessex Poems*. The heaps of burning grass might be a figure for memory or for funeral pyres or commemorative flames at war memorials. They prepare us for that intrusive capitalised word 'Dynasties', which has the din of battle inside it – Christian soldiers, military certainty – when the resonant, capitalised noun hits the ear. Its reverberating din shatters the slow, bucolic silence.

The 'this' that will go onward the same may be the poem itself – poetry's whisper, like love's, will survive, but we know that in the last stanza he's really saying that love and war, like love's strategies and arguments, will always go on. Hardy wrote a ballad on this theme – 'The Sergeant's Song', which he included in a novel he published twenty-five years before he wrote this poem. In *The Trumpet-Major*, we're told:

> When Husbands with their wives agree,
> And Maids won't wed from modesty;

Then Boney he'll come pouncing down,
And march his men on London town!
Rollicum-rorum,tol-lol-lorum,
Rollicum-rorum,to-lol-lay!

We're touched by the maid and her wight whispering their love for each other – against the dynastic noise they're like wisps, leaves blown in the air. But 'annals' intrudes an ugly noun like 'anal' and 'annuls'. The maid and her wight are versions of Hardy and Emma Gifford, who died in 1912. He is remembering their happy youth and long, difficult marriage. Note how the *w* in 'War' and 'will' picks up 'wight', and twists the sound away from the pastoral and personal idyll.

Written in eight-and-six ballad form, this poem asserts that there will always be love and war – as the poets have said, they're versions of each other. The last stanza has four rhymes on *i*, and this places great weight on the last word 'die.'

~

'The Self-Unseeing' is set in the Hardy family's cottage in Lower Bockhampton, on the edge of Egdon Heath. The first stanza refers to the fact that his parents moved the position of the front door and replaced it with a window. The rhythm of the first stanza is subtle and arresting: 'Here is the ancient floor' – a trochee followed by two iambic feet. The next line is a spondee followed by an iamb and an anapaest: 'Footworn and hollowed and thin', with an internal rhyme on *or*. That rhyme is continued in the next line, a trochee followed by two iambs: 'Here was the former door'. The last line is different again: 'Where the dead feet walked in' – a trochee followed by two spondees.

The changing metrical pattern, and the internal rhymes, as well as the internal half-rhyme on 'Foot' and 'feet', give an intent, upward movement to the lines. This is Hardy's rendition of his father's fiddle-playing, which he celebrates in the second stanza (the *o* in 'bowing' picks up the second *o* in 'hollowed'). The second stanza is slow, sad, before the triumphant last line, which conquers death by asserting the memory of the dead.

With hindsight, they were unselfconsciously happy, but the third stanza, which tells us this, cannot sustain the ecstatic momentum of the two previous stanzas:

> Blessings emblazoned that day;
> Everything glowed with a gleam.

The anapaest 'with a gleam' is echoed in the final anapaest, '-ing away'. The rhythm is samey, and although 'emblazoned' puns on the blazing fire, it's an intrusive word out of heraldry. The word clashes with the poem's simple language and with its domestic setting. The final exclamation mark is damaging too.

Thomas Hardy ~ 'Proud Songsters'

The thrushes sing as the sun is going,
And the finches whistle in ones and pairs,
And as it gets dark loud nightingales
    In bushes
Pipe, as they can when April wears,
  As if all Time were theirs.

These are brand-new birds of twelve-months' growing,
Which a year ago, or less than twain,
No finches were, nor nightingales,
    Nor thrushes,
But only particles of grain,
  And earth, and air, and rain.

Hardy placed this poem near the very beginning of *Winter Words,* which he hoped to publish on his eighty-eighth birthday. He died just before it, so the volume was published posthumously. The poem begins with a certain jaded weariness: he is in his eighties, so his sun, too, is sinking. He has seen nine decades of new spring leaves and nesting song birds, and he has read innumerable poems about spring – what else is there to say?

Perhaps he is remembering that more than a decade back he published at the end of *Moments of Vision* one of his finest poems to open with an image of spring. 'Afterwards' begins:

> When the Present has latched its postern behind my tremulous stay
> And the May month flaps its glad green leaves like wings.

The word 'postern' suggests 'posthumous' – he is being put out the back door like a rubbish bin for the refuse cart. But that word 'latched' suggests 'hatched', so the new green leaves are like fledglings, whose flapping wings suggest angels, even happy-clappy angels. He is thinking of resurrection, and a later image in 'Afterwards' – 'Till they rise again as they were a new bell's boom' – brings the resurrection to mind.

'Proud Songsters' begins lazily, without confidence. Those *s* sounds in the first line create an annoying susurrus that carries on into the next line, and the next. This is routine, mechanical, natural process: we have been here many times before, it's a stale subject. He remembers Milton and Keats's darkling nightingale, and he remembers his millennial poem of nearly thirty years before, 'The Darkling Thrush', a title that also picks up Arnold's 'darkling plain', a figure for the clash of ideas and classes in Victorian England. He calls the birds 'loud', which suggests their intrusive, almost vulgar, clashing. He is remembering a piece of prose he wrote more than three decades before:

> The season developed and matured. Another year's instalment of flowers, leaves, nightingales, thrushes, finches, and such ephemeral creatures, took up their positions where only a year ago others had stood in their place when these were nothing more than germs and inorganic particles. Rays from the sunrise drew forth the buds and stretched them into long stalks, lifted up sap in noiseless streams, opened petals, and sucked out scents in invisible jets and breathings.

This is from *Tess of the D'Urbervilles*, and it again describes a routine natural process: the poem in a sense plagiarises his own prose. The first stanza is routine verse, perfectly competent and fluent, but verse nonetheless, and in the shadow of the earlier prose.

The next stanza carries on the memory of the earlier prose description, but now the rhythm becomes more interesting: these are two clumps of three stressed syllables. So 'brand-new buds' and 'twelve-months' growing' adds interest to the fluent, easy rhythm of the first stanza. The next line begins with a cretic foot – 'Which a year' – before shifting back into regular, normative iambic rhythm. In the next line, the archaic word 'twain' sets up echoes with Hardy's poem about the *Titanic* disaster, 'The Convergence of the Twain', and with those convergences of two lovers – with disaster following – that are the main subject of his fiction. The paired finches begin this subject. The stanza form, with that very short fourth line, works cleverly to reduce the finches, nightingales, thrushes almost to nothing. They seem to crowd back into the vanishing point – if this were a drawing – and the penultimate line pursues that reductiveness. Hardy read books about Einstein, whom he mentions in a late poem, and was interested in relativity and particle physics. Also he had read Lucretius, so the structure of the entire universe is glanced at in that apparently innocuous phrase 'particles of grain'. The word 'grain' has nothing but beneficent associations: wheat and corn are golden, celebrated, precious. The line moves nimbly, oiled by that trisyllabic noun 'particles', then the rhythm slows as it moves into a line of monosyllables, which are further slowed by the three commas, then that full stop, which one imagines Hardy setting down with a definite push of the pen nib, its black ink seeding the last particle.

At the very last moment the birds hatch: and out of the *guh* in 'grain' comes the *uh* in 'earth', out of 'rai' in 'grain' comes 'air', and then 'rain' finally splits out of 'grain'. It is a miraculous moment of fertilisation and birth, and part of the miracle lies in the way Hardy has at the very last moment transformed facile verse into poetry. He has surprised us, and this effect is dramatic.

The principle of surprise he defined as 'Gothic' in the chapter in his 'biography', which covers the publication and reception of *Wessex Poems*:

> Years earlier he had decided that too regular a beat was bad art. He had fortified himself in his opinion by thinking of the analogy of architecture, between which art and that of poetry he had discovered, to use his own words, that there existed a close and curious parallel, both arts,

> unlike some others, having to carry a rational content inside their artistic form. He knew that in architecture cunning irregularity is of enormous worth, and it is obvious that he carried on into his verse, perhaps in part unconsciously, the Gothic art-principle in which he had been trained – the principle of spontaneity, found in mouldings, tracery, and such like – resulting in the 'unforeseen' (as it has been called) character of his metres and stanzas, that of stress rather than of syllable, poetic texture rather than poetic veneer; the latter kind of thing, under the name of 'constructed ornament', being what he, in common with every gothic student, had been taught to avoid as the plague. He shaped his poetry accordingly, introducing metrical pauses, and reversed beats; and found for his trouble that some particular line of a poem exemplifying this principle was greeted with a would-be jocular remark that such a line 'did not make for immortality'. The same critic might have gone to one of our cathedrals (to follow up the analogy of architecture), and on discovering that the carved leafage of some capital or spandrel in the best period of Gothic art strayed freakishly out of its bounds over the moulding, where by rule it had no business to be, or that the enrichments of a string-course were not accurately spaced; or that there was a sudden blank in a wall where a window was expected from formal measurement, have declared with equally merry conviction, 'This does not make for immortality.'

This principle he learnt from his work as an architect and from reading Ruskin's chapter 'On the Nature of Gothic' in *The Stones of Venice*. Ruskin urges his readers to examine 'those ugly goblins, and formless monsters, and stern statues, anatomiless and rigid; but do not mock at them, for they are the signs of the life and liberty of every workman who struck the stone'. Ruskin opposes 'engine-turned precision' and links the Gothic with liberty and freedom of thought.

The packed stresses in the opening line of the second stanza are a type of Gothic ornament, whose heaviness sets up a resistance, which the last line effortlessly flies past into the freedom Ruskin celebrates. In late age Hardy is saying, 'I can still practise my Gothic art, I can still sing with these young birds – I am the proudest songster of them all.'

W. B. Yeats ~ 'Sailing to Byzantium'

I

That is no country for old men. The young
In one another's arms, birds in the trees,
– Those dying generations – at their song,
The salmon-falls, the mackerel-crowded seas,
Fish, flesh, or fowl, commend all summer long
Whatever is begotten, born, and dies.
Caught in that sensual music all neglect
Monuments of unageing intellect.

II

An aged man is but a paltry thing,
A tattered coat upon a stick, unless
Soul clap its hands and sing, and louder sing
For every tatter in its mortal dress,
Nor is there singing school but studying
Monuments of its own magnificence;
And therefore I have sailed the seas and come
To the holy city of Byzantium.

III

O sages standing in God's holy fire
As in the gold mosaic of a wall,
Come from the holy fire, perne in a gyre:
And be the singing-masters of my soul.
Consume my heart away; sick with desire
And fastened to a dying animal
It knows not what it is; and gather me
Into the artifice of eternity.

IV

Once out of nature I shall never take
My bodily form from any natural thing,
But such a form as Grecian goldsmiths make
Of hammered gold and gold enamelling
To keep a drowsy Emperor awake;
Or set upon a golden bough to sing
To lords and ladies of Byzantium
Of what is past, or passing, or to come.

This is one of Yeats's finest poems. It begins his volume *The Tower*, which was published in 1928, and has its origins in the ageing poet's anxieties about growing old, the nature of poetry and about his own art. Yeats appears to dismiss 'that country' in less than a full line. He was unhappy with the effect, and in a radio broadcast said it was 'the worst bit of syntax I ever wrote'. The dull iambic line he substituted – 'Old men should quit a country where the young' – does not improve on the arresting opening.

In his 1893 study of Whitman, J. A. Symonds asks: 'is art destined to subside lower and lower into a kind of Byzantine decrepitude, as the toy of a so-called cultivated minority?' The idea that art is a mere plaything, a bauble, a decorative toy, a consumer object, a piece of court jewellery, the property of an elite, perhaps stayed with Yeats. Hazlitt said that Tom Moore had reduced the wild harp of Erin to a musical snuff-box, and Yeats does not want to be the butt of similar accusations. His rhymed metrical verse is so traditional compared with Whitman's free verse that there seems no bond of influence between them. Yet the natural imagery in the first stanza is reminiscent of Whitman and also of his argumentative disciple D. H. Lawrence, whose flawed and foolish novel, *Lady Chatterley's Lover*, Yeats admired. Perhaps Lawrence's free verse had made him anxious about his own poetry? Perhaps the future lies with a Whitmanesque verse of natural impulse and freedom? This may be part of what is nagging him at the beginning of the poem.

The stress on 'old' is strong and emphatic because the adjective takes extra weight from 'no', so that is accented in a pejorative, dismissive tone: 'ōld mēn' is a spondee, not the iambic foot it would be if he had said 'That is a country for old men'. The *uh* sounds in *young one another* exert a retrospective weight on 'country', to make the obvious pun. Here, the effect is assisted by the many *n* sounds in the first three lines. The first line's enjambment assists the sense of haste, which begins with the dismissive, gestural word 'That'. The dash that opens the third line sustains the pace, and the absence of a necessary semi-colon at the end of the line prevents it from slowing down.

Strictly 'salmon-falls' doesn't need a hyphen, but it increases the speed of the phrase while paradoxically making it like the epic compound adjective 'mackerel-crowded', which looks back to Homer's 'wine-dark sea' or 'rosy-fingered dawn'. Both phrases, then, have weight as well as speed and that weight is felt in what they apparently are not – 'Monuments of unageing intellect' – where the *en* picks up *sensual commend generations* and *men*. The stress falls heavily on the first syllable of 'mackerel', like a smacking sound or like fry breaking the surface of the sea, and this draws attention to 'commend', a decorous word out of ritual or court etiquette that elevates nature and the transitory, as does, 'Whatever is begotten born, and dies', which sounds like the language of the Anglican Prayer Book (that language would have been part of the Sligo landscape for Yeats, as his grandfather was the Church of Ireland rector at Drumcliff). Horace in a famous phrase – 'aere perennius' – said his poems would be more lasting than brass, and here Yeats sets the immortality of art against the transience of nature.

But Yeats is wary of being too monumental, so he uses half rhymes – *young/song, trees/seas/dies* – only allowing the full rhyme *song/long*. He then offers a too emphatic rhyme, what Ted Hughes called a 'deadlock rhyme', in the stanza's closing couplet, where the guttural *k* sounds in 'caught' and 'music' impact on 'neglect' and reverberate in 'intellect' in a slightly too grainy, too vibrant manner. The rhymes click shut, and perhaps the *l*s which had oiled the middle lines become too prominent in 'intellect'. Inside 'monument' we can see 'moment' – it's as though he wants to stretch the sensual music of 'Fish, flesh, or fowl', its vigorous speech moment, into eternity. With 'monuments of its own magnificence' he draws down the *o* sound in 'coat' to make a solid wall of sound that feels impregnable.

Yeats places the *n* sound in the penultimate line, and he places it again in the last line, so that *Mon men un in* make clean *n* sounds, unlike *-tions* at the end of 'generations', which we hear as 'shuns', a negative sound that sandwiches *un* between two susurruses. Also *Mon*, with its capital M, is a mountain made plural by the full word's last letter. The spondee 'unage' is plumb in the centre of the line and this gives great permanence to the idea.

The contraction to 'aged' in the next line is dismissive, and this is underlined by 'paltry' and 'thing'. The first two lines are conventionally iambic, but the enjambment on 'unless' hurries the pace, which is then immediately arrested by the spondee 'Soūl clāp'. There is another moment of angst on 'sing', a slight one because we realise that the line isn't quite end-stopped. The repeated dentals in 'tatter' repeat the word and the previous strong *t* sounds to make the noun dance as though it's a verb, and this is a kind of triumph – the rags seem to stand up like leaves or to stretch like the throats of singing birds. It's as though one of Synge's tramps is speaking. Perhaps Yeats was remembering this moment when he completed 'Cuchulain Comforted' on his deathbed with these lines:

> They sang, but had nor human tunes nor words,
> Though all was done in common as before;
>
> They had changed their throats and had the throats of birds.

But this is gentler, resigned, while there is a smacking effect on 'tatter', as there is on 'mackerel'.

In the second stanza, Yeats has used two pairs of full rhymes. He now varies it by rhyming 'studying' with 'sing' – there isn't a full stress on the last syllable of 'studying'. When he reaches 'magnificence', we detect only a chime with 'dress', but in hearing 'sense' in 'magnificence' we perhaps remember 'sensual' before interpreting the ghost word 'sense' as 'meaning' and 'idea' rather than 'physical sensations'. The word 'own' draws down the *o* in 'coat', so that the ragged cloth now feels like sculpture.

Here, Yeats arrives at the riskiest moment in the poem. He has pulled out the rhetorical stops, an action which the word 'of' often signals in an English sentence. Although 'of' is a native English word, it was employed from the eleventh century as the equivalent of the French 'de'. English is blessed with what the Italians call 'the Anglo-Saxon genitive' – 's – and this lends a pacier, more spoken, less formal and rhetorical quality to sentences. As a general rule one 'of' is more than enough in an English sentence, and a line of poetry with 'of' twice is fatally flawed. An exception is the conclusion of Yeats's 'The Valley of the Black Pig':

> We who still labour by the cromlech on the shore,
> The grey cairn on the hill, when day sinks drowned in dew,
> Being weary of the world's empires, bow down to you
> Master of the still stars and of the flaming door.

The *f* sounds in the last line soften the insistent dentals, and the stress that falls on the second 'of' varies the rhythm subtly. But in 'Sailing to Byzantium', Yeats has placed 'of' almost in the middle of the sixth line of this stanza, and he does so again in the last line. This is pushing poetry towards sonorous rhetoric, but worse happens when the couplet completes itself: the '-um' is pulled up too strongly to rhyme fully with 'come' in what is almost literally a bum rhyme which stops the line dead in its tracks.

Yeats, however, is lifting the verse onto a new level, as he takes the *o* from 'holy' and begins the next stanza with 'O sages'. Inside the second word we see 'age', and we remember 'aged'. Then we take 'O' through 'holy' and back to 'old' in the very first line of the poem, and this prepares us for 'gold', which transmutes 'old' into precious, eternal metal, and prepares us for the four repetitions of 'gold' in the last stanza.

Yeats knows he's been a shade, or more than a shade, too monumental, so he moderates the full *gyre/fire/desire* rhyme with the softer *wall/soul/animal*. However, the closing couplet is too strident as the final *ee* in 'eternity' is lengthened and lifted by having to rhyme back to the monosyllable 'me'. The medial 'of' is again rhetorical and portentous, an effect emphasised by the word 'artifice', which has pejorative overtones of 'artificial' and 'sly'. Three times we meet 'of' in this stanza, and that is pushing it. Also the words 'perne' and 'gyre' are a shade too idiosyncratic, too personal and home-made. Yet the *O holy gold holy soul* pattern of assonance is arresting and uplifting. Also the compound word 'singing-masters' right at the centre of the line and the stanza challenges its fecund equivalents in the first stanza.

When the *o* pattern is picked up by 'Knōws nōt whāt', the clacky 'not what' internal rhyme negates the *o* sound poignantly, while the three packed stresses instead of being a powerful molossus communicate a vulnerable quality, which of course is what the phrase 'a dying animal' possesses. Here the process of growing old attains a pitch of grief and helplessness that is intensely tragic. From 'sick' onwards the *ih* sounds are repeated like a hammer hitting nails into a coffin lid.

The word 'nature' at the beginning of the next and last stanza takes great stress on its first syllable because that long *a* sound picks up 'ages' in 'sages' and 'aged'. It also picks up in anticipation the *ay* in 'take'. The *ah* sound in 'natural' visually picks up the first syllable in 'nature' and takes it back to 'not' in the previous stanza to make the adjective negative. This type of sight rhyme makes *form/from/form* triangulate form and insist on the importance of *o*, which is also zero – eternity and nothing – as the poem moves to its conclusion. The rhymes are all full, though with a slight softening of the final syllable of 'enamelling', which is partly because the 'am' sound is made stronger by its internal rhyme with 'hammered'. Yeats knows that he has to find ways of softening emphatic sounds, so the *ow* in 'out' he repeats in 'drowsy', whose second syllable goes back to 'bodily', a word whose initial *b* is repeated in 'bough', which echoes 'drowsy' and brings the physical, the somatic, back into a stanza which seems to be rejecting nature.

Yeats now has another attempt at the *come/Byzantium* rhyme, and this time it's as though he has learnt from the way he muffed it at the end of the second stanza. He sets up an echo of the triple rhythm of the first stanza's 'Fish, flesh or fowl' and 'begotten, born and dies', but he slows the line down by using five monosyllabic words, with a pause at the first comma; then he shifts from iambic rhythm to a foot of three syllables, an amphibrach – 'or passing' – which has the effect of lengthening the iambic foot, then extends that length with a pause before completing the line with a cretic foot – 'or to come' – which just beyond the very last moment rhymes back to 'Byzantium' in a way that seems deferred, held back, still to come, and therefore not really complete. It's as though the final rhyme word is still somewhere in the future. It hasn't arrived yet and therefore can never be over. Thus the rhythms of nature carried over into the last line are eternal, like art. Yeats has fused nature with eternity. He has followed through Blake's gnomic observation that 'Eternity is in love with the productions of time.' The plosive *p* in 'Emperor' is repeated in 'past' and 'passing' to give those words permanence, and perhaps in them we also hear the plosive in 'soul clap its hands'? The last line is also like a refrain in a song – it carries the idea of being repeated again and again, and this also fuses time with eternity. Yeats at the very last moment dramatically throws off the curatorial, the antiquated or antique, and ceases to identify simply with high art. Really that last line is like a refrain in a song – he has gone beyond the chanting rhythm of the third stanza, and the terse dramatic soliloquy of the opening lines of the fourth stanza, to create unhurried space for the unaccompanied human voice.

W. B. Yeats ~ 'In Memory of Eva Gore-Booth and Con Markiewicz'

The light of evening, Lissadell,
Great windows open to the south,
Two girls in silk kimonos, both
Beautiful, one a gazelle.
But a raving autumn shears
Blossom from the summer's wreath;
The older is condemned to death,
Pardoned, drags out lonely years
Conspiring among the ignorant.
I know not what the younger dreams –
Some vague Utopia – and she seems,
When withered old and skeleton-gaunt,
An image of such politics.
Many a time I think to seek
One or the other out and speak
Of that old Georgian mansion, mix
Pictures of the mind, recall
That table and the talk of youth,
Two girls in silk kimonos, both
Beautiful, one a gazelle.

Dear shadows, now you know it all,
All the folly of a fight
With a common wrong or right.
The innocent and the beautiful
Have no enemy but time;
Arise and bid me strike a match
And strike another till time catch;
Should the conflagration climb,

Run till all the sages know.
We the great gazebo built,
They convicted us of guilt;
Bid me strike a match and blow.

Yeats's ear is running with *l* sounds in the opening lines, then with the long *o* in *windows open kimonos*. The pause at the comma allows him to add a fifth long *o* in 'both' without it seeming too much. The dominant sounds are therefore *o* and *l*, and they are attractive, they enhance its aristocratic owners and they enhance the neoclassical mansion – the big house and its estate are near the Atlantic coastline, a few miles from Sligo. But Yeats is also introducing a guttural sound, which begins with 'Great' and is strengthened by 'silk' and 'kimonos'. It appears again in 'gazelle', which anticipates the arresting, deliberately slightly daft word 'gazebo'.

The gutturals set up the passage that refers to Con Markiewicz's death sentence after the Easter Rising in 1916. She was reprieved and went on to become a cabinet minister – the first female cabinet minister in Europe – when the Irish Free State was founded in 1922. This passage uses gutturals, but it drags; the earlier *o* sound has lost its bounce, perhaps because it, too, is lonely. The raving autumn shearing summer blossom is both too dramatic and a cliché. The accent is snobbish and vague – 'the ignorant,' 'I know not' – but the guttural comes back hard and harsh in 'politics', where the *k* seems to take extra emphasis. We note that Yeats has adopted the *In Memoriam* stanza and tetrameter but has, after the first quatrain, over-ridden the expected four-line divisions to create an elegy that looks like a stretched sonnet. There is something disappointing about the phrase 'Some vague Utopia', but the plosive *p* puts weight on 'politics'; still, the poem is in trouble, this is a prosy passage after the arresting and magnificent opening. Then in the next seven lines Yeats gets it all back: typically the *t*s resonate, and 'Many' and 'one or' give a trochaic authority and singing cadence to the lines. The *k*s run from rhyme to rhyme : *politics seek speak mix*, with *Pictures* thrown in as well. This is a firm, scratchy sound, and Yeats's distinctive use of the demonstrative 'that' is felt in 'That table', a spondee with an added unstressed syllable, which arrests and isolates the phrase, then alliterates with 'talk' to isolate the line as representing something wholly wonderful. The word 'youth' half-rhymes with 'both', and it carries a faint memory of the *south/both* half-rhyme at the beginning. He then repeats the third and fourth lines, bringing back the whole opening. He has redeemed the dullness of the 'raving autumn' passage, but it has served its turn because a poem cannot be always elevated, always sublime, it has to have flat passages. Just as acrobats will sometimes appear to make a mistake, so poets know that poems are performances which must now and then seem to put a foot wrong in order to make the words dance perfectly the next moment.

Then Yeats addresses the two dead sisters, and if we take the second line of the poem and place it above this line, we can see how the poem's acoustic memory works:

> Great windows open to the south
> Dear shadows, now you know it all

In the first we have two identical long *o* sounds followed by *ow*, in the second we have *o ow o*, the same sounds in a slightly different order. The effect is to call back the light, the youth, the beauty of the sisters, while simultaneously representing them as ghosts (for years I could not understand why this line always made me choke when I read the poem aloud – until I discovered this particular sound pattern). Yeats can now risk a tendentious statement, and get away with it (the innocent and the beautiful have many more enemies than time). The repeated *i* sounds drive the lines forward, while the *k* sound comes back in 'strike' and 'catch'. It first appeared in 'silk', where the *ih* and the *l* offset its abrasive sound. Yeats is also drawn to the scratchy *ch* sound in 'match' and 'catch', as he contemplates the fact that 'they' – the Irish nationalist majority – believed that all members of the Anglo-Irish Ascendancy shared a historic guilt. The 'great gazebo' here means not just a summerhouse in the grounds of a big house, but the whole rickety, exploitative Ascendancy with its great writers, buildings, orators and fighting spirit. But the last line quite marvellously seems both to lend a punch and throw a feint because that final *o* goes back to 'gazebo' – brings it back – and also plays through the second line again. The great windows open to the south, the dear shadows who know it all, reverberate in 'blow', so that at the very last moment Yeats breathes new life into their memories and reinvigorates their – and his – culture. It's as if he has blown against a dandelion clock and seeded the air with tiny shining filaments for a moment.

W. H. Auden ~ 'Musée des Beaux Arts'

About suffering they were never wrong,
The Old Masters: how well they understood
Its human position; how it takes place
While someone else is eating or opening a window or just
   walking dully along;
How, when the aged are reverently, passionately waiting
For the miraculous birth, there always must be
Children who did not specially want it to happen, skating
On a pond at the edge of the wood:
They never forgot
That even the dreadful martyrdom must run its course
Anyhow in a corner; some untidy spot
Where the dogs go on with their doggy life and the torturer's
   horse
Scratches its innocent behind on a tree.

In Brueghel's *Icarus*, for instance: how everything turns away
Quite leisurely from the disaster; the ploughman may
Have heard the splash, the forsaken cry,
But for him it was not an important failure; the sun shone
As it had to on the white legs disappearing into the green
Water; and the expensive delicate ship that must have seen
Something amazing, a boy falling out of the sky,
Had somewhere to get to and sailed calmly on.

This poem opens with a beautifully confident sentence sound, as Robert Frost calls this vernacular effect. In written prose the statement would be, 'The Old Masters were never wrong about suffering.' Speech changes this into something intimate and tender, and puts the poet and the reader on an equal, communicative level. If Auden had written the line as I have prosed it, he would have sounded pompous, like a smugly assured art critic.

The voice shifts after the first line: the long *oo* in 'understood' is picked up by 'human', which takes extra stress because of it. There is an Anglican preacher here, or a lecturer with a similarly confident, authoritative, ruling-class voice. The language has also become rather abstract and intellectual, and as if to compensate Auden offers a much longer line with twenty-one, not ten syllables, a line packed with quotidian detail.

As a student, I admired this poem, and then I read the American poet and critic Randall Jarrell on Auden, and suddenly all the adjectives and set phrases in several Auden poems stood out like sore thumbs. I began to see that after that assured, very natural – don't let's use 'human' – opening, there is something willed and factitious in the poem. Here, at the end of the 1930s, a decade he was soon to characterise from the safety of New York as 'low' and dishonest', Auden is settling terms with the politics he had espoused.

He begins, unexpectedly, by showing old people as inspired by intense religious passion: they await the miraculous birth – of Christ, of a new state – while the children aren't especially involved. They are both bored and sceptical, but mostly they're at play in their own worlds. Here, Auden works to weave big events into the fabric of daily life, as Samuel Johnson does in a famous passage in his preface to Shakespeare, where he contrasts a man burying a friend with a reveller hastening to the wine-shop. Johnson, the gloomy Tory anarchist, knows that nothing much can be done to change life. Fanciful political schemes only make it more difficult to endure.

Auden seconds this in that slightly campy phrase 'the dreadful martyrdom', which, because it isn't particular, makes the martyrdom run-of-the-mill, routine, not human. Life goes on, the next lines say, ascribing a human value, innocence, to the torturer's horse. The tone is that of insouciant journalism. The Anglo-Saxon, alliterative rhythms of Auden's earlier verse have disappeared, to be replaced by twee adjectives such as 'doggy' and superficial adverbs like 'dully'. The use of 'for instance' belongs to this type of chatty language – it cites the unheroic indifference of ordinary life in the detached manner of a critical essay or a lecture. This is the poet as tourist and connoisseur, someone detached, who can employ the phrase 'not an important failure' as a dismissive, slightly magniloquent wisecrack to characterise Icarus's failure. I see Stephen Spender here, or perhaps any Shelleyan, radical 30s poet.

In saying that the sun shines 'as it had to', he gives the same message as the opening of Ecclesiastes, where the preacher illustrates his theme that all is vanity by saying:

> One generation passeth away, and another generation cometh: but the earth abideth for ever.
> The sun ariseth, and the sun goeth down, and hasteth to the place where he arose.

Life, the poem suggests, rests on the pillars of the powers that be – all ambition to escape like Icarus from the Minotaur's labyrinth is doomed to failure.

But why is the ship 'expensive and delicate'? These adjectives are challenging, and they perhaps designate what Marxists, referring to culture in capitalist society, call 'superstructure'. Trade and the aesthetic objects it generates and pays for is attractive, but what is also attractive to Auden is that ship moving over the ocean. He knows war with Germany is very close, and like Icarus and Daedalus he is looking for a means of escape. On 18 January 1939, he sailed for New York. After the war broke out in September 1939, a question was asked about his departure in the House of Commons, because he was seen as having deserted his country in its hour of need. This poem is an interesting failure, by a writer who went on to become quite an important failure, writing poems in a glossy, metropolitan, intellectually inflected language that read rather like chirpy opinion pieces in the *New Yorker*.

Louis MacNeice ~ 'Order to View'

It was a big house, bleak;
Grass on the drive;
We had been there before
But memory, weak in front of
A blistered door, could find
Nothing alive now;
The shrubbery dripped, a crypt
Of leafmould dreams; a tarnished
Arrow over an empty stable
Shifted a little in the tenuous wind.

And wishes were unable
To rise; on the garden wall
The pear trees had come loose
From rotten loops; one wish,
A rainbow bubble, rose,
Faltered, broke in the dull
Air – What was the use?
The bell-pull would not pull
And the whole place, one might
Have supposed, was deadly ill:
The world was closed,

And remained closed until
A sudden angry tree
Shook itself like a setter
Flouncing out of a pond
And beyond the sombre line
Of limes a cavalcade
Of clouds rose like a shout of

Defiance. Near at hand
Somewhere in a loose-box
A horse neighed
And all the curtains flew out of
The windows; the world was open.

This poem is dated just before the lowest spot in the last war – Dunkirk. The British Expeditionary Force is bogged down in France, and this can be felt in the stagnant look of a vacant house somewhere, I take it, in Ireland, which to MacNeice's anger remained neutral throughout the war.

The opening is tight-lipped, a throwaway remark with a martial alliteration in those two *b*s. The line reminds us of Dickens's *Bleak House* – so it glances at misery, forlorn hope, the absence of justice. The house has a déjà-vu quality, or it may have been visited far back in the past – it's not clear. But the place is dead, and that adjective 'blistered' could carry memories of blistered bodies. MacNeice's generation was haunted by the First World War, and now it is happening again. His short lines are minimalist, constrained, but perhaps influenced by Irish poetry he sets up a spreading pattern of internal rhymes: the *ee* in 'bleak' travels through *been weak dreams*, infecting each word with its bleakness. Similarly, *drive find alive* chime, as do *dripped crypt* and *mould arrow over*, as well as the three *ih* sounds in the last line of the first stanza, which pick up the *ih* in 'tarnished'. Everything is infected, it is both hopeless and claustrophobic: the dripping crypt of the shrubbery – those dark, deathly rhododendrons and laurels – summons a war memorial to mind. This is a return to the past – the ear notices how dominant that *ih* sound is, as *crypt* picks up 'in' and 'blistered' before passing it on to 'tarnished' and to the last line. In MacNeice's poem that ugly, curtailed, short vowel *ih* insists that we are really in it, so that 'wind', whose windiness is denied by 'tenuous', seems to shrink into itself.

We speak of arguments being tenuous, and this adjective communicates a sense of being lost and vulnerable. The syllable 'ten' will appear again in 'rotten'.

The *ih* sound is repeated in the opening of the next stanza – these are wan, feeble wishes, but MacNeice will do something with that *ih* sound later in the poem. Now he underlines the stagnancy of the house and its garden with an allusion to Tennyson's 'Mariana':

> With blackest moss the flower pots
>   Were thickly crusted, one and all:
> The rusted nails fell from the knots
>   That held the peach to the garden-wall.
> The broken sheds looked sad and strange:
>   Unlifted was the chinking latch;
>   Weeded and worn the ancient thatch
> Upon the lonely moated grange.

A line from Shakespeare's *Measure for Measure* – 'Mariana in the moated grange' – is the epigraph to Tennyson's poem, and signals that it was the inspiration behind the poem. Similarly, 'moated grange' and Tennyson's poem spoke to MacNeice as a figure for Britain, the island nation, about to be isolated in the war – the fall of Belgium and France are a couple of months away. That descriptive adjective 'loose', which is repeated in the third stanza's 'loose-box', carries 'lose' with it, because defeat and victory are somewhere in his mind. Defeat is present in 'Faltered', a word on a par with 'tenuous'.

There are mentions in 'Mariana' of the 'crescent-curtain' and the 'white curtain', whose 'gusty shadow' sways to and fro. MacNeice picks up on their movement in his poem, but he draws strongly on the stagnant detail – Tennyson's peach becomes a pear . The pattern of internal rhymes continues, with a particular emphasis on the *o* in 'rose', which passes through *broke whole supposed* to finish in *closed.* (This may echo the mournful double *o* in 'lonely moated', an effect MacNeice wants to blow open.) The combination of the consonant *s* with *o* serves to fur the vowel, and in this context make it slightly mouldy, but we will return to that sound later. Here, it helps create a claustrophobic, predetermined atmosphere, like a derelict graveyard. From 'wall' through *loose loops bubble Faltered dull bell-pull pull whole ill* and the other words with *l* in them there is a descent to *ill* and *closed*. Rainbows usually symbolise hope, but the rainbow bubble is more like gas bubbling from rotten vegetable matter in the pond that is mentioned in the last stanza.

Then he sets a moment of motion or gusto loose, as that 'sudden angry tree' breaks the deterministic fix of the situation and shakes itself like a setter. Here, the hunting dog's vigorous movements break the setness in 'setter'. The gluey internal rhymes are brisker, less insistent now – *angry/tree, Flouncing/out, pond/beyond, line/limes, cloud/shout*. This forces up the lines, as what is in effect a military push takes place: the cavalcade of clouds, the shout of defiance, break the pattern, as does the neighing horse, which seems to kick in unison with the curtains blowing out of the windows in what is an image of birth, or rebirth.

That *ih* sound, so dominant in the middle stanza, is cleanly revived in the last line's 'windows', which contains the verb 'win' (the consonant *n* draws out the vowel). The *oh* sound furred by *s* is repeated in 'windows', but MacNeice bats *o* out again in the very last word 'open', where the plosive *p* stretches the sound out and lifts it up. We hear 'hope' in 'open', so this is a victorious line – demoralisation and dullness have been cast off.

Keith Douglas ~ 'Canoe'

Well, I am thinking this may be my last
summer, but cannot lose even a part of
pleasure in the old-fashioned art of
idleness. I cannot stand aghast

at whatever doom hovers in the background;
while grass and buildings and the somnolent river,
who know they are allowed to last for ever,
exchange between them the whole subdued sound

of this hot time. What sudden fearful fate
can deter my shade wandering next year
from a return? Whistle and I will hear
and come another evening, when this boat

travels with you alone towards Iffley:
as you lie looking up for thunder again,
this cool touch does not betoken rain;
it is my spirit that kisses your mouth lightly.

Keith Douglas commanded a tank group in the main assault on the Normandy beaches on the 6 June 1944. Three days later, near the village of St Pierre, he was killed in action. He was twenty-four years old. He had joined the army immediately war was declared in September 1939, while he was a student at Oxford. His enlistment was deferred and he returned to Oxford. In 1940 he joined a cavalry – i.e. tank – regiment and fought in the Battle of Alamein in October 1942. He wrote a brilliant prose memoir, *Alamein to Zem Zem*, about that battle.

In 'Canoe' he adopts Tennyson's *In Memoriam* stanza, which rhymes ABBA. Where Tennyson wrote his elegy for Arthur Hallam in lines of four iambic feet – tetrameters – Douglas chooses lines of mainly five feet, pentameters. And he chooses 'Canoe' as title, though the small boats on Oxford's rivers are either rowing boats or punts. Perhaps he was thinking of these lines from Eliot's *The Waste Land*, where a woman remembers a sexual encounter:

> 'Trams and dusty trees.
> Highbury bore me, Richmond and Kew
> Undid me. By Richmond I raised my knees
> Supine on the floor of a narrow canoe.'

Sex and love are on Douglas's mind, as he addresses a young woman and imagines his punt – unusable word – returning to the river, which the classical word 'shade' (*manes* in Latin) suggests is also the Styx or the Channel, which he will later cross on D Day.

He begins conversationally – 'Well, I am thinking' – and displays a relaxed confidence by breaking the first four lines unexpectedly on adjectives and prepositions. The dominant or nodal sounds he's setting up are first introduced by 'I' and 'thinking'. The *ih* sound in 'Iffley' is repeated in 'in', then *i* appears twice in the next line. There are three *ih* sounds in the next stanza, two in the next stanza, along with two *i* sounds. Then in the last stanza there are a total of nine *ih* sounds and three *i* sounds: the *i* sounds triangulate as 'lie' in the second line of the concluding stanza is echoed in 'my' and 'lightly' in the last line. We catch an echo of 'Iffley' in 'lightly', because the *l*s echo each other: both are bisyllabic words with the stress on the first syllable. The *ih* sound derives from Iffley, an attractive village on the river just south of Oxford. 'Iffley' has a ghostly sound, and it contains 'if'. As Douglas would have known, Rupert Brooke's 'The Soldier' begins:

> If I should die think only this of me –

> There is a corner of a foreign field
> That is forever England.

Here, 'I' and 'die' match each other.

But Douglas would also have known that Kipling has a famous poem entitled 'If':

> If you can keep your head when all about you
> Are losing theirs and blaming it on you;
> If you can trust yourself when all men doubt you,
> But make allowance for their doubting too.

Deep down in his acoustic memory, he is bracing himself for a conflict, which will lead to his death. Iffley carries the question 'if I should die'. His poem is altogether gentler and subtler than those of his patriot predecessors. He sets up the idea of 'ghost' in 'aghast', and then uses the Anglo-Saxon word 'doom' to imply the idea of battle, perhaps even glance at Auden's 'Doom is darker and deeper than any sea dingle'. That verb 'hover' perhaps picks up Auden's early poem 'Missing', which begins:

> From scars where kestrels hover
> The leader looking over
> Into the happy valley.

The 'grass and buildings and the somnolent river' in Douglas's poem turn Christchurch and its meadow into the happy valley threatened by war. He repeats another nodal sound, the *o* which is first introduced in 'old' and repeated in *somnolent know whole boat alone betoken* . This *o* sound is paralleled by the *oo* sound in 'lose', which is repeated in *Doom looking cool*, and in the title 'Canoe'. The *o* sound in 'no', is negative, but it gives way to 'cool', before falling back into 'betoken rain', a figure for the war, death, tears, that then gives way to the tactile last line, where their lips touch and his 'I' springs back at the very last moment. The phrase 'fearful fate', is in

'Iffley' – those *f*s reverberate in the gently ominous name – while his wandering shade suggests Aeneas, who descends into the underworld in Book Six of the *Aeneid*, and who wanders in search of a new kingdom. It is the repetition of sound which gives this poem its tactile texture: the *t*s in the last stanza pick up on the last *t* in 'boat' at the end of the third stanza, and become concentrated in 'lightly', so that we sense the tips of their tongues touching, and catch the delicately erotic in 'spirit' and 'kisses', words whose liquid *s*s touch each other with a tiny hint of spittle.

His lover was Antoinette Beckett, who was a fellow undergraduate. She quickly earned distinction for her work in ULTRA, the top secret military intelligence radar operation for which she was mentioned in despatches. She was one of the few people privy to the ULTRA secret, which broke the German war code. She married a highly decorated South African pilot, Group Captain David Haysom, and lived most of her life in South Africa, where she was active in Black Sash, a group of women who held silent protests against apartheid. Her son Nicholas, a constitutional law expert, helped draw up the new South African constitution. She died in 1999 in Warwick, aged seventy-nine. She and Douglas had a stormy relationship, which she finally ended when she told him she could stand his jealousy no longer. 'Canoe' was first published in May 1940.

Robert Lowell ~ 'Sailing Home from Rapallo'

Your nurse could only speak Italian,
but after twenty minutes I could imagine your final week,
and tears ran down my cheeks . . .

When I embarked from Italy with my Mother's body,
the whole shoreline of the *Golfo di Genova*
was breaking into fiery flower.
The crazy yellow and azure sea-sleds
blasting like jack-hammers across
the *spumante*-bubbling wake of our liner,
recalled the clashing colors of my Ford.
Mother travelled first-class in the hold;
her *Risorgimento* black and gold casket
was like Napoleon's at the *Invalides*. . . .

While the passengers were tanning
on the Mediterranean in deck-chairs,
our family cemetery in Dunbarton
lay under the White Mountains
in the sub-zero weather.
The graveyard's soil was changing to stone –
so many of its deaths had been midwinter.
Dour and dark against the blinding snowdrifts,
its black brook and fir trunks were as smooth as masts.
A fence of iron spear-hafts
black-bordered its mostly Colonial grave-slates.
The only 'unhistoric' soul to come here
was Father, now buried beneath his recent
unweathered pink-veined slice of marble.
Even the Latin of his Lowell motto:

> *Occasionem cognosce,*
> seemed too businesslike and pushing here,
> where the burning cold illuminated
> the hewn inscriptions of Mother's relatives:
> twenty or thirty Winslows and Starks.
> Frost had given their names a diamond edge. . . .
>
> In the grandiloquent lettering on Mother's coffin,
> *Lowell* had been misspelled *LOVEL*.
> The corpse
> was wrapped like *panettone* in Italian tinfoil.

Lowell arrived at the hospital in Rapallo shortly after his mother died. He stayed with a friend, Blair Clark, at Neuilly on his way to Rapallo. Clark recalled: 'I had the feeling that he should immediately have gone to Rapallo if he wanted to see his mother alive, but he didn't.' He was in the early stages of an attack of manic depression. To Elizabeth Hardwick, his wife, he wrote: 'Pretty rough. I spent the morning with her nurse, who speaks Italian, both of us weeping and weeping. I mean I spent it in the room with her body!'

Some months later, he wrote a piece of prose about his mother's death:

> I arrived at Rapallo half an hour after Mother's death. On the next morning, the hospital where she died was a firm and tropical scene from Cézanne: sunlight rustled through watery, plucked pines, and streaked the verticals of a Riviera villa above the Mare Ligure. Mother lay looking through the blacks and greens and tans and flashings from her window. Her face was too formed and fresh to seem asleep. There was a bruise the size of an ear-lobe over her right eye. The nurse who had tended Mother during her ten days dying, stood at the bed's head. She was a great gray woman and wore glasses whose diaphanous blue frames were held together with a hair-pin. With a flourish, she had just pulled aside the sheet that covered Mother's face, and now, she looked daggers at the body, as if death were some sulky animal or child who only needed to be

frightened. We stood with tears running down our faces, and the nurse talked to me for an hour and a half in a patois that even Italians would have had difficulty in understanding. She was telling me everything she could remember about Mother. For ten minutes she might just as well have been imitating water breaking on the beach, but Mother was alive in the Italian words. I heard how Mother thought she was still at her hotel, and wanted to go walking, and said she was only suffering from a little indigestion, and wanted to open both French windows and thoroughly air her bedroom each morning while the bed was still unmade and how she kept trying to heal the haemorrhage in her brain by calling for her little jars and bottles with pink plastic covers, and kept dabbing her temples with creams and washes and always, her quick cold bath in the morning and her hot aromatic bath before dinner. She kept asking about Bob and Bobby. "I have never been sick in my life." *Nulla malattia mai! Nulla malattia mai!* And the nurse went out. *Qua insieme per sempre.* She closed the door and left me in the room.

That afternoon I sat drinking a cinzano with Mother's doctor. He showed me a copy of Ezra Pound's *Jefferson and/or Mussolini*, which the author had personally signed with an ideogram, and the quotations, '*Non . . . come bruti . . .*'

Lowell helped to organise a small Episcopalian service in Rapallo's English chapel. He had bought 'a small black and gold baroque casket that would have [been] suitable for burying her hero, Napoleon at Les Invalides'. He said that the undertakers misspelled his mother's name on the coffin as *LOWEL*. 'While alive Mother had made a point of spelling out her name letter by letter for identification. I could almost hear her voice correcting the workmen. "I am Mrs Robert Lowell of One Seventy Marlborough St. Boston, L,O,W,E, *double* L."'

He wrote this account some months after her death, but in a letter to Blair Clark just a few months after she died he has the misspelling as 'Charlotte Winslon'. In his prose he describes the journey back to the States:

On the Saturday morning when we sailed, the whole shoreline of the Golfo di Genova was breaking into fiery flower. A crazy Piedmontese

> Baron raced about us in a parti-coloured sea-sled, whose outboard motor was, of course, unmuffled. Our little liner was already doing twenty knots an hour, but the sea-sled cut figure-eights across our bows. Mother, permanently sealed in her coffin, lay in the hold. She was solitary, just as formerly, when she took her long walks by the Atlantic at Mattapoisett in September, which she called "the best season of the year" after the summer people had gone. She shone in her bridal tinfoil, and hurried homeward with open arms to her husband lying under the White Mountains.

The poem is taking shape in the prose, and in an early draft of 'Sailing Home from Rappallo' he writes:

> The young, very au courant hospital doctor
> Owned a presentation copy
> Of Ezra Pound's *Cantos*.
> Worried by my hypo-mania
> He gave me a bottle of chlorpromazene.

Lowell's manic depression is part of the poem's subject – this is the contribution biography makes to the study of this uneasy, imperfect poem.

Lowell begins by blaming the nurse for not being able to speak English. The third line seems thrown in casually for the rhyme, and this jars. Also he is describing, not enacting grief.

The next line is slightly gauche, because normally one embarks *for* not *from* a place. Lowell admired Dryden, and he may have remembered the uses of the verb in his great translation of the *Aeneid* (at the end of Book Six, Aeneas 'Embarqu'd his Men, and skim'd along the sea'). The verb imparts to Lowell something of the quality of an epic hero. In an epic, the phrase 'fiery flower' could denote the enemy massing on the shoreline, but here it is a figure for Lowell's mania.

The sea-sleds, adapted from the one he observed, also figure his mania: they are 'crazy', a word which chimes with the slightly odd, heraldic word 'azure', and which he uses of the Piedmontese baron in the letter ('blue' in Italian is *azurro*). Lowell was much obsessed by family – the Lowells and Winslows were ancient Boston families – and 'azure' is the ground of the genealogical structure he is going to erect in the poem. He ironises this ambition slightly, when he says that his mother travelled 'first-class in the hold'. This is the second example of a favourite and obsessive formation in Lowell: the compound word. In this poem, we have: *spumante-bubbling, first-class, deck-chairs, sub-zero, spear-shafts, black-bordered, grave-slates, pink-veined.* Reading through Lowell's *Collected Poems*, I find several hundred examples of hyphenated words. He even writes 'car-park'.

Perhaps Lowell is thinking of his early poem, 'Falling Asleep over the Aeneid', as he sets sail from Rapallo:

> The sun is blue and scarlet on my page,
> And yuck-a, yuck-a, yuck-a, rage
> The yellowhammers mating. Yellow fire
> Blankets the captives dancing on their pyre,
> And the scorched lictor screams and drops his rod.
> Trojans are singing to their drunken God,
> Ares. Their helmets catch on fire. Their files
> Clank by the body of my comrade – miles
> Of filings! Now the scythe-wheeled chariot rolls.

Later, he writes of a 'wild bee-pillaged honey-suckle'. For him, the compound adjective or compound noun is the stuff of heroic poetry – he writes 'sky-line' not 'skyline'. This feature owes a lot to Yeats, who creates a heroic poetry through it – 'world-famous, golden-thighed, Pythagoras'; 'blear-eyed wisdom'; 'O chestnut-tree, great-rooted blossomer' ('Among Schoolchildren'). These are all versions of Homer's wine-dark sea, but when Yeats mentions Shawe-Taylor in 'Coole Park and Ballylee, 1929', one begins to trace a double-barrelled, Anglo-Irish identity coming through. The hyphen is a cultural bridge, and is fundamental to the Boston Brahmin, Lowell.

He is fascinated by energy and violence now, just as he was as a schoolboy – *breaking blasting bubbling clashing*. All these verbs have what Hazlitt defined as 'gusto'. They embody 'passion or power defining an object'. The aesthetic form he is thinking of is baroque: those azure sea-sleds have a baroque energy, and they also bring the blue of heaven into the picture, as well as precious stones. So they are like angels on an Italian baroque ceiling. Looking back at 'embarked', I wonder if it doesn't begin the baroque theme? That verb is picked up by 'breaking'.

Lowell associates his mother with liberty – the Italian Risorgimento, that nineteenth-century movement for Italian unification that culminated in the establishment of the kingdom of Italy in 1861. And he associates his mother with her hero and his obsession, Napoleon. Napoleon's body was brought back in 1840 from St Helena to lie in state in the palace known as the Invalides.

Lowell's mother, we at some level know, has died an invalid, but he is now making her into a hero, and associating her with a Parisian palace. The spondee 'first-class' insists on her importance even though we know there are no class divisions in a ship's hold. There is a Jack Yeats painting called *The Island Funeral* which shows a coffin on the deck of a yawl travelling to the Aran Islands – it is a parable of emigration, and at some level Lowell's poem is about the American relationship with Europe. The austere, northern family cemetery contrasts with the hedonistic south: there is an epic insistence in the black brook and the fir trunks 'smooth as masts' – travel again. Trunks are containers, like suitcases. And those trunks are hidden in 'embarked'. Lowell is brandishing his own, in many ways neo-imperial style, when he writes:

> A fence of iron spear-hafts
> black-bordered its mostly Colonial grave-slates.

The half-rhymes *drifts/masts/hafts/slates* give a monumental density to the lines, and this has been prepared for by the graveyard soil changing to stone. The presence of the *Aeneid* – another settler culture – can be felt here, and Lowell's naval father is shown to be unworthy of it because 'pink' carries the idea of cowardice. His Latin motto is also ironised, but we still know that there is a family motto, an aristocratic 'distinction'.

Lowell was very concerned with literary pre-eminence, asking a graduate student in the early 1960s, 'Is Frost still first?' In this poem, he would have known that the noun 'Frost' would act as a pun, conferring with 'diamond' a particular New England distinction.

As in his remark about his father's Latin motto seeming 'too businesslike and pushing', the adjective 'grandiloquent' seems to allow the idea of grandiloquence into the poem by apparently denying it. We return to linguistic misunderstanding, as Lowell adapts the undertakers' original mistake to *LOVEL*, which puts love in capital letters, but slightly inarticulately. He smuggles the emotion in without really saying it or expressing it, but it is nevertheless there. And the image of her corpse being 'like *panettone*' is tactile, loving, with the idea of resurrection and communion inside it. Its bad taste is also baroque. Also the last word 'tinfoil' gives a lift to 'coffin', bouncing as it does off 'Italian' and 'panettone'. The final *l* rhymes with 'LOVEL', and this serves to give significance to that nonce word. And the run of plosive *p*s in the last line give energy to 'corpse' – we are back staring at the liner's '*spumante*-bubbling wake'. Though Lovell overuses italics in the poem, he does let them give an angelic lift to the lines. They come to possess what Hopkins calls 'the roll, the rise, the carol, the creation'. We might expect 'marble' after 'Italian', but this is light, flickering, airy metal, like silver leaf or angels – it takes us back to that precious word 'azure'. But it is also 'in' that feminine colour 'pink' and establishes a last-minute communication between his soft failure of a father and his formidable mother. It also, by association, brings the slice of marble back – marble sliced like bread. The marble is 'pink-veined' like a living face, we realise. And so the poem comes together at the last moment. What had always seemed to me an imperfect poem changed when I began to write about it, and an altogether finer structure started to reveal itself.

Zbigniew Herbert ~ 'Elegy of Fortinbras'

Now that we're alone we can talk prince man to man
though you lie on the stairs and see no more than a dead ant
nothing but black sun with broken rays
I could never think of your hands without smiling
and now that they lie on the stone like fallen nests
they are as defenceless as before The end is exactly this
The hands lie apart The sword lies apart The head apart
and the knight's feet in soft slippers

You will have a soldier's funeral without having been a soldier
the only ritual I am acquainted with a little
There will be no candles no singing only cannon-fuses and
bursts
crepe dragged on the pavement helmets boots artillery horses
drums drums
I know nothing exquisite
those will be my manoeuvres before I start to rule
one has to take the city by the neck and shake it a bit

Anyhow you had to perish Hamlet you were not for life
you believed in crystal notions not in human clay
always twitching as if asleep you hunted chimeras
wolfishly you crunched the air only to vomit
you knew no human thing you did not know even how to
breathe

Now you have peace Hamlet you accomplished what you
had to
and you have peace The rest is not silence but belongs to me
you chose the easier part an elegant thrust

but what is heroic death compared with eternal watching
with a cold apple in one's hand on a narrow chair
with a view of the ant-hill and the clock's dial

Adieu prince I have tasks a sewer project
and a decree on prostitutes and beggars
I must also elaborate a better system of prisons
since as you justly said Denmark is a prison

I go to my affairs This night is born
a star named Hamlet We shall never meet
what I shall leave will not be worth a tragedy

It is not for us to greet each other or bid farewell we live on archipelagos
and that water these words what can they do what can they do prince

[*translated by Czeslaw Milosz*]

This classic political poem is dedicated to the famous Polish poet Czeslaw Milosz, who translated it into English. Milosz renounced Communism, while Zbigniew Herbert was always deeply opposed to it. We might think this is about Shakespeare's Hamlet, but it is that figure and play as they were perceived by generations of Poles which is the subject of the poem.

Hamlet was staged for the first time in Poland two years after the country lost its independence in 1797. The actor who played Hamlet and who directed the play, Wojciech Boguslawski, had been a prominent participant in the Kosciuszko Insurrection three years earlier. In this production, Denmark became Poland and Claudius the three monarchs – Catherine the Great, Maria-Theresa, Frederick – who partitioned the country between Russia, Prussia and Austria.

Then there was a version of *Hamlet* called *Horsztynski*, a historical drama written by Juliusz Slowacki in the 1830s. The Polish critic Jan Kott describes it:

> This Polish Hamlet, Szcesny-Kossakowski by name, is the central figure of the play. He has a fine aristocratic lineage; his father commanded the Polish army and his uncle was a bishop. Both the father and uncle are authentic historical figures. Both were hanged during the Koscuiszko Insurrection.

The first Hamlet in Polish drama is torn between the old nobility of Poland and the 'mob of tailors and cobblers', who are rebelling against Russian imperialism.

Hamlet was a favourite figure in the early 1900s. He carried the burden of Polish history, read Nietzsche and the Polish romantic poets, and knew it was his duty to struggle for the liberation of his nation.

Herbert's poem is about Hamlet the Polish idealist, and it is also about the way art and the artist can seem to intervene – or try to intervene – in politics. Herbert has no illusions about such interventions, and he has no illusions either about the politicians who hold power and shape the state.

Hamlet was produced in Cracow in 1956, during the 20th Congress of the Soviet Communist Party in Moscow, which took place three years after the death of Stalin and just before the political thaw, which followed Khruschev's famous speech to that Congress denouncing Stalin's crimes. The play was political from start to finish, Rosencrantz and Guildenstern behaved like secret police agents, and 'To be or not to be' meant 'To act or not to act', because this prince was both an angry young man and a rebellious communist.

Reading Herbert's poem, we can see that it is on one level about the contradiction between political idealism and political pragmatism or ruthless political action (sometimes these two forms of action are similar, sometimes not). The image of the 'black sun with broken rays' goes back to *Samson Agonistes* – 'O dark, dark, dark, amid the blaze of noon' – and is used by the great Russian poet Osip Mandelstam, who died in one of Stalin's concentration camps (he wrote the famous Stalin ode denouncing the dictator as the Kremlin mountaineer). Mandelstam has a recurrent image of the sun being buried at midnight. The black sun also echoes Gérard de Nerval's 'El Desdichado': 'le soleil noir de la mélancolie'.

That image of Hamlet's hands being like fallen nests is touching and delicate, and it must be a memory of the passage in *Macbeth* where Macbeth notices the martens' nests on the walls of Duncan's castle:

> No jutty, frieze,
> Buttress, nor coign of vantage, but this bird
> Hath made his pendent bed and procreant cradle.

The nests give Hamlet a gentle, vulnerable quality: he is characteristically defenceless, rather than a young man with a sword.

But who is Fortinbras? We can make our own connections, but in any political context he embodies two clichés – 'the bottom line' and 'at the end of the day'. He is nothing if not a realist. Perhaps he will reform the prison system? Or perhaps he will build bigger prisons and fill them with more and more detainees? In British politics, he is often played by the Home Secretary.

Fortinbras knows that Hamlet's state funeral will be an excellent propaganda opportunity, which will help create the myth of Hamlet, that 'star named Hamlet'. His canonisation will assist Fortinbras's control of the state. Herbert's Fortinbras is both a soldier and a politician, but at moments his voice has a lyric cadence that makes him more than the tough, terse man of action and cynical operator:

> but what is heroic death compared with eternal watching
> with a cold apple in one's hand on a narrow chair
> with a view of the ant-hill and the clock's dial

The cold apple may be the apple of the tree of knowledge – Fortinbras is not a philistine or an ignoramus (Stalin, we may recall, was a singer, a former seminarian, and widely cultured).

The closing lines of the poem are religious in their cadence and texture:

> It is not for us to greet each other or bid farewell we live on archipelagos
> and that water these words what can they do what can they do prince

These beautiful lines have a trailing incompleteness reminiscent of the opening of Eliot's 'Marina', and of its closing lines:

> What seas what shores what granite islands towards my timbers
> And wood thrush calling through the fog
> My daughter.

In the end we wonder if Fortinbras sounds romantic and mystical, not armour-plated? Perhaps he, too, has succumbed to the dream and the myth. He and Hamlet are kin, they need each other.

Patrick Kavanagh ~ 'Kerr's Ass'

We borrowed the loan of Kerr's big ass
To go to Dundalk with butter,
Brought him home the evening before the market
An exile that night in Mucker.

We heeled up the cart before the door,
We took the harness inside –
The straw-stuffed straddle, the broken breeching
With bits of bull-wire tied;

The winkers that had no choke-band,
The collar and the reins . . .
In Ealing Broadway, London Town
I name their several names

Until a world comes to life –
Morning, the silent bog,
And the god of imagination waking
In a Mucker fog.

The first rude, deliberately provincial word in Kavanagh's masterpiece 'Kerr's Ass' occurs in the title. It's repeated in the first line: 'We borrowed the loan of Kerr's big ass', where there is a back-formation out of Irish, a phrase which is normal in Irish speech but in print could look clumsy to an outsider, who might regard borrowing a loan as tautological or a malapropism. Again 'ass' can mean 'bum' – it does so exclusively in American English – so the appearance of rude provincialism is emphasised by the first line.

Kavanagh wants to put oral convention in conflict with conventional standard – to set up a tension between spoken Irish English and correct printed English. The long vowels in *we borrowed loan* have an almost elocutionary plumminess against the short, jabby vowel sounds, and the guttural, plosive and susurrus in 'Kerr's big ass'. Kavanagh wants to raise McGonagall's homemade ghost – he's being cute – and he wants the Scotch-Irish surname and its *k* sound to become nodal. So that *k* is replicated in *exile Mucker Cart broken winkers choke collar Mucker*. The softer guttural *g* in 'big' is also replicated – it adds density to *k* – till the two come together in the triumphant final phrase, 'Mucker fog'.

The other rude word is 'Mucker', a place name which derives from the Irish 'muck' for 'pig'. Mucker is a place where pigs are bred in abundance, but it is an ugly name, and the inhabitants of Kavanagh's Mucker agitated unsuccessfully for it to be changed to 'Summerhill'.

If *k* or *kuh* is a nodal sound in the poem, so is *uh*, which we first hear clearly in 'Dundalk', which means 'fort of Dealgan'. It is then furred and aspirated in 'butter', or 'buhter' or 'buhtur' (Kavanagh on tape pronounces 'bull-wire' as 'buhllwire'). This *uh* sound is an ugly internal rhyme, part of the poem's rudeness or deliberate naiveté – and Kavanagh offers an immediate half-rhyme in the next line, where 'him home' trips the line up slightly.

The exilic theme begins in the fourth line, but is immediately denied by the parochial Mucker, which bogs it down in the mud, because 'muck' also obviously means muck, clay, clabber, even as 'ass' could imply shite. The two *i* sounds in 'exile' and 'night' are cancelled by 'Mucker'. But Kavanagh wants to introduce a long *ee* sound, which he doubles in 'we heeled', a slightly clumsy consonance. Then he repeats 'we' and brings the *i* sound back with 'inside'. He wants to put 'we' and *i* in relation to each other, maybe to merge himself with the parochial and the communal, maybe to distinguish himself from it.

Now he lobs a tongue-twister at the reader: 'The straw-stuffed straddle, the broken breeching' – the long *ee* positively squeaks there and becomes ugly, like a breach in nature. Also this is the moment when the story-teller becomes particular and technical – he wants to hold our attention by boring us. And he adds the extra detail of the bull-wire, which has the effect of bringing a powerful animal slightly into the picture and intensifying that *uh* sound both by repetition and association. The *i* sound is put under pressure here – there'll be no escape from this ugly place, a place he's tied to. And he adds yet more detail which increases the claustrophobia, even though the choke-band is notionally not there. This is the cunning naive imagination patiently detailing the facts – the recycled objects that make the harness and the poem. From the point of view of the literary theorist Kavanagh is a *bricoleur* here – a second-hand dealer who if he were Yeats would recycle sea green slates and old bits of metal.

Then the long clean *ee* sound comes back as Kavanagh shifts into perfectly modulated, proper English:

> In Ealing Broadway, London Town
> I name their several names.

There's the ghost of 'healing' in 'Ealing', and this crosses the gap that the three dots make, like hands across the Irish Sea. To adapt Muldoon, he is meeting the English. He is putting the prominent phrase 'London Town' wittily into the picture, as though it's a big village not a city – again this is a vernacular phrase which plays against the higher style of these two lines.

But the language is heightened, ritualistic, proper: 'I name their several names.' Like a chant, the line elevates not *straddle breeching bull-wire winkers choke-band,* but the primal act of naming objects which 'their' makes human, creaturely. That 'sever' in 'several' is over-ridden by another act of joining, of participation, as the penultimate stanza flows effortlessly into the last stanza and repairs the broken breeching. The movement is now open, revelatory: the dash doesn't introduce the deliberately clumsy 'straw-stuffed straddle' or 'broken breeching' but 'Morning, the silent bog', a cadence which calls back 'Ealing Broadway, London Town'. The word 'bog', though, does call back 'butter', 'broken breeching', 'bits of bull-wire', and it carries a faintly derisive tone and meaning – asses, after all, are placed on bogs, on jakes. Then, in a version of Coleridge's infinite I AM, the god of imagination is shown waking – the present participle at the line end creates a pause and sense of expectation, before the final line which combines bathos with elevation and renewed devotion to place. We notice 'in' three times in the last two lines, which helps emphasise the subject of dwelling-in-the-world – what is sometimes called the ontological subject. There is a slight pause before 'waking', which gives power and strength to the verb. Also 'In a Mucker fog' is trochaic – it picks up the trochee 'Morning' and this imparts an elevated, ritualistic tone, even as 'fog' and 'bog' set up a counter-bathos so that the poem at the end seems to both rise and sink. The words 'under', 'butter', 'bog' and 'fog' all create a sinking squelchiness, which is the opposite of the dry factuality of the straddle, breeching, bull-wire. Somewhere in 'Mucker fog' there could ever so slightly be a trace of 'motherfucker', and certainly 'Mucker' at some level implies the dismissive 'fucker'.

Ted Hughes ~ 'Thistles'

Against the rubber tongues of cows and the hoeing hands of
men
Thistles spike the summer air
Or crackle open under a blue-black pressure.

Every one a revengeful burst
Of resurrection, a grasped fistful
Of splintered weapons and Icelandic frost thrust up

From the underground stain of a decayed Viking.
They are like pale hair and the gutturals of dialects.
Every one manages a plume of blood.

Then they grow grey, like men.
Mown down, it is a feud. Their sons appear,
Stiff with weapons, fighting back over the same ground.

Against. This is a poem about opposition, recalcitrance – the again and again of conflict. Ted Hughes was born in Yorkshire and grew up in the Calder Valley, historically one of the centres of the Industrial Revolution. He was brought up a Protestant dissenter, and that experience shaped his imagination – he chooses the free way, not the formal, as Oliver Cromwell did. He is uncomfortable with rhyme and regular metre; his ear is keyed to Anglo-Saxon alliterative verse, which is present in 'holding hands' and in the repeated guttural *k* sounds. The 'rub' in 'rubber' speaks for the pressure he admires – he dislikes smooth surfaces.

That dislike is reflected in those *k* sounds in the first stanza: 'spike', 'crackle', 'black'. They bring warfare into the poem: guns are spiked, guns crackle, as does gunpowder, and 'blue-black' is close to gunmetal blue. That last compound adjective is drawn from 'The Windhover', by one of Hughes's favourite poets, Hopkins:

> No wonder of it: sheer plod makes plough down sillion shine,
> And blue-black embers fall, gall, and gash themselves gold-
> vermilion.

That phrase 'blue-black embers' is caught up in 'blue-black pressure' – the *eh* sound is common to the nouns in both phrases.

Towards the end of his life, Hughes returns to it again in 'The Beach', with its memory of Sylvia Plath:

> The sea moved near, stunned after the rain.
> Unperforming. Above it
> The blue-black heap of the West collapsed slowly,
> Comfortless as a cold iron stove
> Standing among dead cinders
> In some roofless ruin.

Hughes said of Plath's poems that they had a sense of 'emergency', and the crackling thistles create such a feeling of emergency. Blue-black is also the colour of bruising, which adds to the sense of pressure. The *ack-ack* repetition in the third line brings a gun almost literally into the poem's frame, and three *k* sounds caught up by 'resurrection' collide – as do 'burst', 'fistful', 'first' and 'thrust'. And they all hit against each other, as do the *ih* sounds in 'fistful' and 'splintered'.

It's as though this is a version of the Greek myth of the dragon's teeth springing up out of the ground as armed men. But this isn't ancient Greece, it's Northern Europe, a Gothic not Classical culture. The poem, we assume, is set in his native Yorkshire, not in Scotland. This is race memory, ethnicity, though the assonance *stain/decayed* puts pressure on that idea, at least as an unambiguous good. That word 'stain' picks up the *st* in 'burst', 'fistful', 'frost' – it signifies strength, but that is dissipated in 'decayed', which keeps the long *a* in 'stain' but drops the *st* sound. This may be why the tone and rhythm change into a tender and gentle cadence. But why is their hair 'pale'? We never say of anyone that they have pale hair. Pale face, pale skin, yes, but never hair. 'Blond' is the adjective we apply to hair. Not here, though.

It may be that it is the very unexpectedness of 'pale' that makes this line so gentle. It is an expected adjective – if Hughes had written 'blond' the poem would be in deep Aryan trouble. But he doesn't, so the thistles cannot be mistaken for stormtroopers.

That phrase 'the gutturals of dialects' brings back into play all the *uh* sounds in the first two stanzas: *rubber tongues summer under pressure one revengeful burst resurrection fistful thrust up*. We also hear 'Icelandic' and 'Viking' in 'dialects', so that after the lightness of 'pale hair' that phrase 'the gutturals of dialects' takes on added weight and significance. Here, Hughes is signalling his early immersion in the dialect of West Yorkshire, and the way it linked him to Middle English poetry. Behind this poem is the experience of coming from a marginal society, where dialect is spoken.

The word 'manages' is curious. Heaney uses it in 'Broagh', where the *gh* sound is 'difficult to manage'. Here, 'manages a plume of blood' means 'succeeds in wearing a crested helmet'. Perhaps Hughes chose the word because it has 'man' and 'ages' in it – he is concerned with manliness and tradition. But 'blood' is close to race memory and ethnicity – we are in risky territory.

In the next stanza 'man' becomes 'men', and 'age' becomes 'grow grey'. This is a 'feud', but can it be a blood feud? Perhaps it is the English Civil War that is being represented, or the endless political struggle between those who hold the hoes, hold power, and those who do not. At the centre of the poem is Hughes's admiration for the indomitable fighting spirit of the British. He edited a selection of Keith Douglas's poetry, and wrote a powerful introduction. In 'Vergissmeinicht' Douglas says:

Three weeks gone and the combatants gone
returning over the nightmare ground
we found the place again, and found
the soldier sprawling in the sun.

That phrase, 'the nightmare ground' is behind 'the same ground', and in 'fighting' we hear both 'Icelandic' and 'Viking', hear the ancestors calling. Similarly 'stiff' calls back 'fistful' and 'splintered', which make it strong, as it also picks up the *st* in the previous two stanzas. This is not a poem in praise of the stiff upper lip, but there is a curious silence at its heart, except that this is the English language speaking, the vernacular, with its local dialect energies fighting back against the standard language. Neither side will win; the life of the language depends on it.

Philip Larkin ~ 'Cut Grass'

Cut grass lies frail:
Brief is the breath
Mown stalks exhale.
Long, long the death

It dies in the white hours
Of young-leafed June
With chestnut flowers,
With hedges snowlike strewn,

White lilac bowed,
Lost lanes of Queen Anne's lace,
And that high-builded cloud
Moving at summer's pace.

A week before Larkin wrote this poem in the summer of 1971, he made this note in his workbook:

White/ Nettle flowers/ White lilac/ Clouds/ Cow parsley/ Daisies

The first stanza reproduces this chipped style of notation: it has a Middle English terseness and simplicity, but Larkin is also thinking of another Hull poet, Andrew Marvell, who in 'Upon Appleton House' writes:

With whistling scythe, and elbow strong,
These massacre the grass along:
While one, unknowing, carves the rail,
Whose yet unfeathered quills her fail.

Larkin's 'frail' combines 'rail' and 'fail', and noticing this we see that there is pain and failure in what might otherwise seem a straightforward adjective describing fragile blossom. We note that there is vulnerability and weakness in the word.

Larkin concluded 'Vers de Société', written two weeks before, by saying:

> Beyond the light stand failure and remorse
> Whispering *Dear Warlock-Williams: Why, of course.*

The words 'ail' and 'fail' are also inside 'frail' in 'Cut Grass'; these associations help to concentrate the theme of transience, failure and death. Paradoxically, 'frail' is strong with various meanings and associations. Also he rhymes 'breath' with 'death', and employs the ugly and intrusive Latinate 'exhale' as a rhyme for 'frail'. The verb has associations with cigarette smoking, and carries the anxieties smokers know. It also carries the idea of exit, expulsion, breath being pushed out – last gasp – and leads naturally into the fourth line, whose *l*s repeat its terminal *l*. There is a miniature massacre in the Marvell lines, which shadows Larkin's implicit mowed field – this is a battlefield like the 'stubble plain' in Keats's 'To Autumn'.

The phrase 'white hours' first struck me as beautiful, the opposite of 'dark hours' or 'black hours', but knowing Frost's 'Design' – 'I saw a dimpled spider thick and white' – I'm not so sure that it is simply and unambiguously beautiful. Perhaps there's a sheeted ghost somewhere in the phrase? The *i* in 'dies' carries over into 'white', and skews the word.

The compound adjective 'young-leafed' is Yeatsian, like the 'sun-comprehending glass' in Larkin's 'High Windows', and he repeats this epic effect in 'high-builded', where there is probably a memory of Prospero's final 'cloud-capped towers' speech. There is a conscious, even heritage archaism in the poem: 'snowlike strewn' is an inversion. There is a chestnut, a 'great-rooted blossomer', in Yeats's 'Among Schoolchildren', so there is another memory here. Also Larkin may be thinking of some English popular festival here –

Derby Day perhaps – or he may be thinking of VE Day, 8 May. There is an idea of victory here, and also of tradition. This is Merry England, and it seems appropriate that the name of the last Stuart monarch should be involved in a risky, slightly camp moment. We associate the phrase 'Queen Anne' with a particular style of house, so there is a combined idea of royalty and domestic, traditional architecture here – the high roofs of such houses are perhaps present in 'high-builded'. But the effect is Shakespearian – the cloud moves like a stately Elizabethan ship, whose aristocratic highness contrasts with the lowness of the cut grass. Gently and firmly, the English class-system, with which Larkin had no quarrel, infiltrates the language and imagery of the poem.

Larkin grieved at Britain's loss of empire, and that high-builded cloud, with the word 'dead' inside it, carries that sadness as the cloud moves slowly towards disintegration – the ship might almost be a Spanish galleon. It is as if the cloud is heading towards those lost lanes of archaic and forgotten customs and traditions. The word 'bowed' carries the idea of age and defeat, even though the lilacs are gloriously white with blossom, and it seems to follow naturally from that uncomfortable inversion 'snowlike strewn'. The word 'strewn' is often used of bodies on a battlefield, and is an ugly word to rhyme with 'June'. The phrase carries three strong stresses, as does 'yōung-lēafed Jūne' and 'Quēen Annē's lāce' – an impacted effect, which is only exceeded by the four stresses in the first line. There is a faraway cricket match in that final noun 'pace', and the whiteness in the poem abets this, but on another level this is a condensed lyric about the slow death of Old England, as well as about his own mortality. The word 'high' links it to the volume's title poem, 'High Windows', where he observes young students in the 1960s and guesses they're having the promiscuous sex denied to him. The word for Larkin carries associations with the high calling of the poet, and with his high position in a lonely tower above the masses.

John Montague ~ 'All Legendary Obstacles'

All legendary obstacles lay between
Us, the long imaginary plain,
The monstrous ruck of mountains
And, swinging across the night,
Flooding the Sacramento, San Joaquin,
The hissing drift of winter rain.

All day I waited, shifting
Nervously from station to bar
As I saw another train sail
By, the *San Francisco Chief* or
Golden Gate, water dripping
From great flanged wheels.

At midnight you came, pale
Above the negro porter's lamp.
I was too blind with rain
And doubt to speak, but
Reached from the platform
Until our chilled hands met.

You had been travelling for days
With an old lady, who marked
A neat circle on the glass
With her glove, to watch us
Move into the wet darkness
Kissing, still unable to speak.

This love poem begins confidently, with those *l*s that mean but do not state 'love', a word that's hidden inside 'glove', three lines from the end. The long adjective 'legendary' in the title, emphasised by its repetition in the first line, suggests an ambition to become famous lovers, star-crossed perhaps, like Romeo and Juliet. But in an Irish poem, 'legendary' summons ancient myth, the past. When we reach 'imaginary' we hear 'legendary' inside it, and realise that it is a grander word than 'imagined', which, strictly, ought to be in its place.

The lovers' meeting took place in 1956, and the poem was published in 1965. There is a song – a lay – in the verb 'lay', which brings to mind a famous song by Bob Dylan:

> Lay, lady, lay, lay across my big brass bed
> Stay, lady, stay, stay while the night is still ahead
> I long to see you in the morning light
> I long to reach for you in the night
> Stay, lady, stay, stay while the night is still ahead.

That big brass bed is a dated piece of 60s furniture, and unlike Montague's poem there are no obstacles, no impediments, here. That low word 'lay' is an obvious double entendre, which ever so slightly infiltrates Montague's use of the verb.

The line break enforces a gap between the two lovers, who occupy both the real world of trains, timetables, station bars, platforms, oil lamps, actual plains, mountains and rivers, as well as the legendary, imaginative reality of love, difficult love. Those 'great, flanged wheels' bring both worlds together – the wheels are indisputably real, but by calling them 'great' Montague lets Yeatsian language and ambition into the poem. We are not going to see Pallas Athene – Maud Gonne – at Howth Station, but we are not far from the same heroic territory.

The bisyllabic 'between', which picks up the *ee* at the end of 'legendary', actually seems to clamp this pair, this twain, together, but the pause at the end of the line makes a gap, a drop. The four syllables of 'legendary' are fully voiced and they stretch the word out. The prominence which 'between' has at the end of the first line seems to clamp this pair of lovers – this twain converging – rather than to separate them; on the other hand there's that gap, that pause. It's then that Montague drops the uncomfortable monosyllable 'ruck' into lines that have so far been lissom with bisyllabic words and with two grand polysyllables. It's an ugly, crowded, hasty word – bedsheets are sometimes described as 'rucked'. The creased effect is unsettling, while the noun 'ruck' means a large number or mass, especially, my dictionary says, of 'ordinary undistinguished people or things'. Like all lovers, these lovers feel special, feel singled out.

The guttural *k* in the pejorative 'ruck' is magnified by the guttural in 'obstacles'. It's an untidy, scrummy word, 'ruck', not too far from 'fuck'. We're going to hear those gutturals in the last stanza in 'mar*k*ed' and 'spea*k*,' and more softly in '*gl*ove'. But the pace changes with the uplifting 'swinging' in the next line (best to avoid a 60s echo here). But the double *ih* sound in 'swinging' becomes uncomfortable in *hissing drift winter*. Before this happens, the *uh* sound in 'ruck' is turned and elevated by 'Flooding' – same sound, but those two *o*s and the sweeping sense of blessed present process, which the participle communicates, change the feeling entirely. It's hard not to hear 'sacrament' and 'sacred' in 'Sacramento', as we catch his nervous, contradictory emotions, his great but mixed expectations.

The name 'Sacramento' designates both the river and the state capital, a city which had suffered devastating floods and fires in the previous century. Petrarch's sonnets imagine love as freezing fire and burning ice, and both 'Sacramento' and 'San Joaquin' embody this figure. But the image of birth – waters breaking – is primary here, while the texture of the language is excited, dangerous, highly strung. The sacred is present again in 'San' – saint – but 'Joaquin' – 'Jokane' – has a dragging guttural that echoes 'obstacles' and 'ruck'. There is a saint here, yes, but there's also a name that sounds like 'Joe

Kane', like a gunfighter almost. Or like Cain. This is a low point emotionally, as we catch the invisible rhyme 'pain'. And that *ay* sound is repeated almost immediately in 'day' and 'waited', just as 'drift' is echoed in 'shifting' before the *ay* rings out in *station train sail Gate great.*

This pained sound is changed by the impression of fabulous size, which the names of the trains communicate: the 'San Francisco Chief' sounds like the name of a legendary native American chief. San Francisco , the city, signifies freedom, sexual freedom, while its great bridge, the Golden Gate, signifies love, a precious wedding ring perhaps, the gateway to Edenic love (though a huge gate is also an obstacle). We are going to see an ephemeral ring – a wedding ring – in the neat circle the old lady will mark with her glove. We are back in the territory of the heroic, and this is underlined by 'Golden' and 'great'. But the circle is also connected with the great flanged wheels, because the adjective 'flanged' has as one of its primary meanings 'attached'. The wheels are still, but only for a short time, because wheels suggest fortune, change, chance. Very soon they'll be reflected in that neat circle, which, like the wheels, is motionless. The steel wheels are still, but only for a short time. In Greek mythology Ixion was punished by Zeus for attempting to seduce Nephele: he was tied to an ever-revolving wheel entwined with snakes, or, in some versions of the myth, to a wheel of fire. Montague has suggested that the myth of Orpheus is in the poem, but I'm unable to see the connection.

There's the faintest hint of another text in 'dripping', which takes us back to 'hissing drift'. Reflecting on the word, I begin to see the dripping tree under which Gabriel Conroy in James Joyce's seminal story 'The Dead', sees the shades of the mighty dead:

> The tears gathered more thickly in his eyes and in the partial darkness he imagined he saw the form of a young man standing under a dripping tree. Other forms were near. His soul had approached that region where dwell the vast hosts of the dead.

But it is the combination of falling water and the word 'great' which takes me to the powerful, slightly sinister epiphany at the end of Robert Frost's 'The Most of It':

> But after a time allowed for it to swim,
> Instead of proving human when it neared
> And someone else additional to him,
> As a great buck it powerfully appeared,
> Pushing the crumpled water up ahead,
> And landed pouring like a waterfall,
> And stumbled through the rocks with heavy tread,
> And forced the underbrush – and that was all.

Here, and in Montague's poem, there is an overwhelming force of a physical manifestation that is also like an annunciation. It is a moment of destiny, one of those moments in your life when you can feel the dangerous future pressing on the present. With its 'heavy tread', Frost's buck is something between an aroused soldier and a tank, and one notes 'ruck' in Montague, 'crumpled' in Frost. In both poems, as in Joyce's ironically inflected prose, a mythological imagination has displaced the realistic narrative of objects and events.

In the next stanza, the *o* in 'negro' picks up the run of *o* signs – signs not sounds – that began with 'obstacles'. They are all leading to that neat circle on the glass. The *l* in 'pale' picks up the *l* in 'flanged', and softens the *ay* sound so dominant in the previous stanza. There is no mention of love in the poem, but it is ghosted in 'Above' and in 'glove' – the love and sexual desire in the poem is suppressed or repressed, and probably all the more powerful for being so. In 'chilled' there is death, lack of love, as well as those hard, cold, *ih* sounds from the first stanza, which converge on 'Until' before the sound is passed on. The 'wet darkness' is also rebarbative and ominous.

The old lady – that *o* again – in an Irish poem has to be a version of Mother Ireland, Cathleen ni Houlihan, ancient and traditional wisdom, but here she is the lover's travelling companion, a passing friend, who marks a circle almost like a sniper taking aim, for she is the future as much as the past. The *g* in 'glass' gives emphasis to 'glove', which has the effect of ever so slightly detaching the *g* to isolate 'love', so that perhaps we notice the last three letters in 'Move' and the soft assonance, which gives touch and texture to the gloved fingers making the circle, a zero which is everything and nothing. The susurrus, which begins with 'days' and then reappears in 'glass', then splits between 'still' and 'speak' and brings the flooding wetness back. It looks like a happy ending with the lovers reunited, but 'still' carries those cold *ih* sounds and 'unable' those pained *ay* sounds, while 'speak' rhymes far back to 'between' at the end of the first line. Surely there is some disaster ahead?

Derek Mahon ~ 'A Disused Shed in Co. Wexford'

Let them not forget us, the weak souls among tbe asphodels.
– Seferis, *Mythistorema*, tr. Keeley and Sherrard

(for J. G. Farrell)

Even now there are places where a thought might grow –
Peruvian mines, worked out and abandoned
To a slow clock of condensation,
An echo trapped for ever, and a flutter
Of wild-flowers in the lift-shaft,
Indian compounds where the wind dances
And a door bangs with diminished confidence,
Lime crevices behind rippling rain-barrels,
Dog corners for bone burials;
And in a disused shed in Co. Wexford,

Deep in the grounds of a burnt-out hotel,
Among the bathtubs and the washbasins
A thousand mushrooms crowd to a keyhole.
This is the one star in their firmament
Or frames a star within a star.
What should they do there but desire?
So many days beyond the rhododendrons
With the world waltzing in its bowl of cloud,
They have learnt patience and silence
Listening to the rooks querulous in the high wood.

They have been waiting for us in a foetor
Of vegetable sweat since civil war days,
Since the gravel-crunching, interminable departure
Of the expropriated mycologist.

He never came back, and light since then
Is a keyhole rusting gently after rain.
Spiders have spun, flies dusted to mildew
And once a day, perhaps, they have heard something –
A trickle of masonry, a shout from the blue
Or a lorry changing gear at the end of the lane.

There have been deaths, the pale flesh flaking
Into the earth that nourished it;
And nightmares, born of these and the grim
Dominion of stale air and rank moisture.
Those nearest the door grow strong –
'Elbow room! Elbow room!'
The rest, dim in a twilight of crumbling
Utensils and broken pitchers, groaning
For their deliverance, have been so long
Expectant that there is left only the posture.

A half century, without visitors, in the dark –
Poor preparation for the cracking lock
And creak of hinges. Magi, moonmen,
Powdery prisoners of the old regime,
Web-throated, stalked like triffids, racked by drought
And insomnia, only the ghost of a scream
At the flash-bulb firing-squad we wake them with
Shows there is life yet in their feverish forms.
Grown beyond nature now, soft food for worms,
They lift frail heads in gravity and good faith.

They are begging us, you see, in their wordless way,
To do something, to speak on their behalf
Or at least not to close the door again.
Lost people of Treblinka and Pompeii!
'Save us, save us,' they seem to say,

'Let the god not abandon us
Who have come so far in darkness and in pain.
We too had our lives to live.
You with your light meter and relaxed itinerary,
Let not our naive labours have been in vain!'

This poem was first published in 1973. The Troubles in the north of Ireland claimed 237 lives that year (thirty years later the death toll stood at over 3,000). Mahon's poem was immediately recognised as a classic, as a very subtle and finely tuned response to a violent political situation that was then in its most vicious phase.

It is dedicated to the novelist J. G. Farrell, whose novel *Troubles* is set in a southern Irish hotel during the war of Independence, which was concluded by the Anglo-Irish Treaty of 1922, an agreement which partitioned the island into the Irish Free State and the State of Northern Island. The epigraph from the modern Greek poet George Seferis distances the poem from Ireland and also introduces a classical dimension. Mahon is not interested, as Yeats was, in writing a country-house poem: he chooses an old shed in a burnt-out hotel, a ruin from a previous cycle of political violence, and is perhaps influenced by MacNeice's 'Order to View'. The words 'shed' and 'shade' are cognate, so 'shed' assonating with 'asphodels', which grow in the underworld, takes us down to both the past and the dead. And as the shed is burnt-out, we see the 'ash' in 'asphodels', and associate it with the death camps.

Mahon is drawn to states of being – stillness, the life of the spirit, art – rather than to history and politics, which are represented here by the lorry changing gear at the end of the lane. The sight chime between 'now' and 'grow' in the first line expresses this static state of being, and the two *th*s in 'there' and 'thought' are reversed in the *ht* which completes 'might' and 'thought', so that a sense of harmless growth and contraction are communicated in what is a classical alexandrine, a line of six mainly iambic feet, with the caesura after 'places' and the reversed iambic foot 'where a'. The reversing of the foot places strong stress on 'where' and introduces the idea of 'air.' This perfectly pitched, apparently spontaneous line has atmosphere. Then 'grow' is echoed by 'slow', and 'Peruvian' slightly by 'echo' – that *eh* sound – before the *oo* in 'Peruvian' is picked up by 'disused', just as 'echo', far off, is repeated in 'Wexford'. There is a guttural *k* in every line except the fifth, which is softened by the repeated *fs*, just as 'grow' softens the guttural. The bone burials were initially 'shit burials', but dogs don't bury their shit, so the word was changed. It would have played against the *ih* in 'rippling' and introduced unease, but 'bone' does this too, and its *o* picks up the previous *os*. It also alliterates tersely with 'burials'.

The star in the next stanza sets up the Holocaust theme, and also the dream of the Promised Land. These are victims of history, survivors, shades, vegetable ghosts, passive witnesses to the departure of the expropriated mycologist. The repeated 'Elbow room!' parodies the inter-war German slogan *Lebensraum* and takes us back into history, just as the phrase 'old regime' does. So this poem witnesses to historical change, from the perspective of the losers.

That phrase 'ghost of a scream' paralleled by the 'flash-bulb firing-squad' brings Munch's famous painting *The Scream* to mind, also Goya's *The Third of May*, which shows a French firing-squad executing Spanish civilians. The *fs* at this point, beginning with 'triffids', an imaginary plant taken from John Wyndham's almost-forgotten science fiction novel *The Day of the Triffids*, pick up the 'flutter/ Of wild-flowers in the lift-shaft' in the first stanza.

But the flash-bulbs also begin the theme of aesthetic anxiety, of running the risk of looking at political violence from the viewpoint of what Seamus Heaney, in a self-incriminating phrase, calls an 'artful voyeur'. This is present in the clever pun 'light meter', where 'light' is both adjective and noun. Read as a noun it refers to a device now incorporated inside cameras, but which used to be a separate object employed by photographers to measure light. Read as an adjective, it refers to light verse, to self-admiring, trivial rhyming. This is the poet as tourist, a role Mahon is repudiating through the final demand made by the mushrooms. A poem, too, can be a naive labour, can look home-made, and this highly sophisticated poem draws the naive and the primitive into itself at the last minute in order to offset its own sophistication, its carefully wrought stanzas, half and full rhymes, patterns of assonance, elegantly pitched lines.

This is a tragic, poignant poem, both gentle and authoritative – it carries suffering with it, and manages to avoid the self-conscious persona of poet commenting on the Troubles: '"Let the god not abandon us/ Who have come so far in darkness and in pain"'. It leaves us to read current events into it, and at the same time indicts us as relaxed consumers, tourists on an old – and new – battlefield. Behind it stand the *Aeneid, The Divine Comedy, Paradise Lost*: it repeats their descents into the underworld in miniature, as with classical piety it gives lasting form to the recent dead in the north of Ireland and to the dead of history.

Seamus Heaney ~ 'Broagh'

Riverbank, the long rigs
ending in broad docken
and a canopied pad
down to the ford.

The garden mould
bruised easily, the shower
gathering in your heel mark
was the black O

in *Broagh*,
its low tattoo
among the windy boortrees
and rhubarb-blades

ended almost
suddenly, like that last
gh the strangers found
difficult to manage.

In 'Broagh' the word 'boortree', which is a dialect corruption of 'bower tree' for 'elderflower tree', is a rude or uncomfortable nodal word. It immediately brings both 'boor' and 'Boer' to mind, so that it is at once local, familiar, comforting, tribal, and clumsy, alien, all that is the opposite of inclusive. Also it picks out the long *oo* sound in 'tattoo'. Behind it is the dialect word 'river broo', which means the shelf-like bank, which the river has undercut. The Irish word *bruachar* means 'brink' or 'edge'. In 'Broagh' there is the idea of a society that is on the brink of total chaos (the early 1970s, when the poem was written and published, were the worst years of the Northern Irish Troubles, with hundreds of murders, thousands of attacks and injuries). The word 'broke' – demotic for penniless – is also inside the title. In a sense this is a poem about the breaking of a nation or a people. Broagh is a place close to Bellaghy, the farm where Heaney grew up in Co. Derry.

There is a drumbeat, that 'low tattoo', inside 'boortrees', and we remember Heaney's poem about the Lambeg drummer's tribal music making the air pound like a stethoscope. The language of the poem has a paradoxical sense of exclusion and inclusion: 'mould' is an English dialect word for 'soil' brought over by seventeeth-century English Protestant planters. The word 'docken' is a Middle English plural form, like 'shoon', and it is commonly used in Northern Irish speech. The Scots word 'rigs' means 'fields'. This is inclusive, deliberately so, but at the end of the poem Heaney plays with the common Northern Irish belief that only the inhabitants of the province can pronounce the *gh* sound in *lough sheugh Broagh*. The British – the strangers in the house of this poem – find that sound, like the province, and before that the whole island, 'difficult to manage'.

What the possible rudeness of 'windy boortees' does – there's the ghost of a fart, of angry public speeches in that phrase – is to amplify the idea of discomfort and anxiety, which is created by traces of deliberate bad taste and embarrassment in the poem. The word 'rigs' is uncomfortable, possibly because we speak of elections being rigged, more because it suggests something temporary and makeshift. The opening word 'Riverbank' is echoed in 'broad docken', so that the phrase is foregrounded, making 'docken' sound final, finished, over-and-done-with, like a boat docking. The word 'docken' is often consciously relished when it's spoken in the North of Ireland, as if the speaker is conscious that it's an unusual word, an archaic usage that has gone native.

The word 'pad' is English dialect for 'path', but there's something stealthy, even sinister in it – we remember 'footpad', an old Elizabethan word for 'thief'. And in any case, the noun 'pad' denotes something slightly ugly and stealthy and to be avoided if possible. But the adjective attached to it, 'canopied', is full-vowelled, rather magnificent. In *Henry IV, Part Two*, King Henry speaks of the 'canopies of costly state', and in Sonnet 12 Shakespeare speaks of 'lofty trees' which 'erst from heat did canopy the herd'. The word is impressed with political, with state power – that and terrorist violence is the real hidden subject of this subtle, ominous poem. Together 'canopied' and 'pad' create a dissonance, as a low word clashes with a high word. The two plosives and the two *d*s arrest the movement of the lines, before the second *d* takes us to 'Down to the ford', where the initial *d* is repeated by the final consonant to insist that we are deep down somewhere, as though on the banks of the Styx.

The *d*s are repeated in the next line, where the word 'mould', though it means soil, and good soil too, because friable, carries connotations of fungus, of death and decay. The word 'mould' is always voiced in a slightly disgusted way, and the verb 'bruised' develops the ugly theme. Then something beautiful and gently erotic happens, as the – we assume – woman's heel makes a 'black *O*', another bruised effect, but a perfect form. Even so a black *O* could be a figure for the formless infinite void, as this poem peers into the political abyss. And '*O*' rhymes with 'Broagh' and with 'low' to reinforce the sinking effect, which begins with 'down to the ford' and is emphasised in the heelmark. The sound of 'Broagh' crosses the *o* sound with a guttural reverberation, like thunder or an explosion. The rhubarb-blades develop the military implication in 'tattoo' – there is violence, rooted, autochthonous violence, in this place. If we consider rhubarb, there's always a stagnant look to clumps of wild rhubarb, but the word itself is uncomfortable, and is a term of derision, which fits with the fact that this poem is a declaration of linguistic independence. It is about reaching the end of one process and beginning another. And at the end the *d* in 'found' is passed on to 'difficult' – we are down even deeper. A small, local Ulster landscape has given us a glimpse of hell.

With its linguistic shifts, its irony and use of uncomfortable words and cadences, Kavanagh's 'Kerr's Ass' and the several mentions of boortrees in his poetry have helped shape this poem, which, in Kavanagh's terms, beds itself in the parish, without being provincial, though it risks the provincial in that long drawn-out word 'boortrees', ugly as 'hoor', the Ulster pronunciation of 'whore'. The subject of 'Broagh' is the very worst of times, and it expresses history and politics through a form of derelict pastoral. This is a bruised, a broken landscape, and 'tattoo' begins the theme of bruising and printing, which works against the wet vaginal *O*.

Before this poem was published, the word 'Broagh' probably existed only in print on an ordnance survey map, so Heaney's poem has brought it from ordinary speech to the printed page. This is a poem which expresses deep anxiety about the present and the future of the Northern Irish situation, it has a terse beauty in the unforced manner with which it confronts the place and its name.

Paul Muldoon ~ 'Quoof'

How often have I carried our family word
for the hot water bottle
to a strange bed,
as my father would juggle a red-hot half-brick
in an old sock
to his childhood settle.
I have taken it into so many lovely heads
or laid it between us like a sword.

A hotel room in New York City
with a girl who spoke hardly any English,
my hand on her breast
like the smouldering one-off spoor of the yeti
or some other shy beast
that has yet to enter the language.

Muldoon's celebrated sonnet 'Quoof' might be regarded as a reply to 'Broagh'; certainly it exists in a dialogue with it. One of the cultural effects of the Troubles can be seen in the way that words normally found only in speech have entered the printed language. This division between orality and literacy is on one level replicated in that black *O* in 'Broagh'. The heelmark is print, but what it signifies is orality, like the exclamation *O!*

Words which belong to speech are family words – in the North of Ireland 'scaldy' and 'docken' are used instead of 'fledgling' and 'dock leaves', or, say, 'mischeevious' and 'ridiklus' instead of 'mischievous' and 'ridiculous'. When these words are used the speakers are bonding with each other if they both belong to the province. But with family words, we know that we must not take them outside the family – no one would understand or care about them, and it would be wrong to try and make strangers understand them. Outside the family, such words are rude, embarrassing, slightly tacky; we must keep them in a kind of purdah.

In 'Quoof', Muldoon suggests that he has taken the Muldoon family word for hot water bottle into many strange beds. There is guilt, anxiety and transgression in this. That transgression is subtly amplified by the condom-like image of the 'red-hot half-brick' juggled and jiggled into an old sock. And the word 'red-hot' suggests sex and danger, even as his father's childhood settle brings innocence and tradition into the poem – the household gods his son has offended.

The half-brick – or 'halver' as they're known in the North, where they were frequently chucked in riots – is an unstable signifier like the word 'quoof', which is close to 'spoof', to 'quim' and to 'loofah', this last an always odd, jokey word. In a way, it's an explosive word, but softly textured as the long *oo* and final *f* soothe the guttural *k*. By using it outside the family, Muldoon has made it into a rude word. His discomfort is there in the comparison he makes to a sword, which like the rhubarb-blades signifies violence, as well as here marital division and the refusal of sex.

This uncomfortable subject is amplified by the comparison of his hand on her breast to the 'smouldering one-off spoor of the yeti'. By employing a word naturalised in English from Afrikaans, Muldoon signifies unease and discomfort. The word means not only 'trail', but with 'smouldering' it remembers the red-hot half-brick, as well as suggesting a warm turd. That word 'spoor' picks up 'boortree' in 'Broagh', which also, as I say, brings the Afrikaners – i.e. bigoted Protestants – into the frame.

Immediately, Muldoon puts 'quoof' back into the category of innocence in the last two lines, but effectively the word has entered the language: it exists now in a printed, public text, and so can never recover its private innocence – that 'enter' is phallic. What we admire in this poem is its one-off certainty and achievement: it rhymes 'City' with 'yeti', and 'English' with 'language', making the speaker into an English-speaking imperial male as he lays his hand on the breast of the unnamed girl who hardly speaks any English. In a way, he takes that identity back when he compares his possessive hand to 'some other shy beast', but like 'canopied pad' in 'Broagh' this is an uncomfortable combination. It joins the gentle to the feral to introduce another imaginary monster or fiction or trick, because the whole poem may be a spoof.

As in 'Kerr's Ass' there is a combination of the local and the familial, because both poems are about emigration, language, identity. The word 'spoor' and the image of a steaming turd that is applied to it is a nodal, rude word in the sonnet, and indeed like 'boor', it shares a long *oo* sound with both 'quoof' and 'rude'. In the first version of the poem, Muldoon wrote 'An hotel room,' which is correct standard English – again, this is like the Ealing Broadway moment in 'Kerr's Ass', but he later made it more familiar and colloquial by dropping the 'n'. In Kavanagh's poem, the mention of Broadway brings in New York, an image of fame and artistic success. 'Quoof' silently or obliquely counts the cost of such success.

Craig Raine ~ ‘ Flying to Belfast’

It was possible to laugh
as the engines whistled to the boil,

and wonder what the clouds looked like –
shovelled snow, Apple Charlotte,

Tufty Tails . . . I enjoyed
the Irish Sea, the ships were faults

in a dark expanse of linen.
And then Belfast below, a radio

with its back ripped off,
among the agricultural abstract

of the fields. Intricate,
neat and orderly. The windows

gleamed like drops of solder –
everything was wired up.

I thought of wedding presents,
white tea things

grouped on a dresser,
as we entered the cloud

and were nowhere –
a bride in a veil, laughing

at the sense of event, only
half afraid of an empty house

with its curtains boiling
from the bedroom window.

The first line is deliberately academic, a gesture of detachment. Old-fashioned or, as it's known, 'traditional' literary criticism sometimes contains sentences that begin 'It is possible to wonder'. Raine starts with this type of anxious but witty and self-conscious donnishness. He laughs – possibly – like the bride later in the poem. That laughter is held at arm's length in the opening line, which avoids a direct admission of nervous laughter, though the word 'possible' is weak, so that the line lacks a natural vernacular pitch.

Then follows the accurate and arresting comparison of aeroplane engines revving up to a kettle whistling on the boil. This is an acoustic image of danger – we apply the image of boiling to anger and to unstable political situations. In Seamus Heaney's 'Churning Day' there is a 'plumping kettle' – a rapidly boiling kettle – and four earthenware milk crocks like 'large pottery bombs'. The political infiltrates the domestic in this early poem. Raine knows that he is flying into an unstable political situation, where random acts of violence take place. Fear of flying and fear of Belfast's violent streets come together here, but he displaces it with three hypothetical images of clouds. The third image – Tufty Tails – is whimsical, but nappies are domestic like Apple Charlotte. That fluffy pudding is a processed organic thing, and he is interested in the process by which the imagination absorbs and transforms nature. If he had mentioned that the clouds looked like ice cream, he would have been invoking Wallace Stevens's grandiloquent subject, his central theme of the aesthetic imagination (this is the subject of one of his most famous poems, 'The Emperor of Ice Cream'). Stevens is deep in this poem, but he is a concealed presence. Part of Raine's anxiety is that he is flying from a culture which teaches that poetry is pure imagination and transcends society and politics, to a different society that doesn't make that separation. It is the 'shovelled snow' image that begins this symbolist theme.

Snow shovelled is nature processed and transformed like the

apples, but is also an oblique allusion to one of the most famous Northern Irish poems – Louis MacNeice's 'Snow', where a living-room window is suddenly 'big' with swirling snowflakes. This is on one level an image of the urban crowd – MacNeice wrote the poem in the 1930s and wanted to give the domestic scene a subtle social resonance.

Raine is also alluding to a poem by a later northern Irish poet, Derek Mahon, called 'The Snow Party', which begins:

> Basho, coming
> To the city of Nagoya,
> Is asked to a snow party.
>
> There is a tinkling of china
> And tea into china,
> There are introductions.

The snow and the tea cups are drawn into Raine's poem, which like Mahon's uses a series of *o* sounds as a structural device. Mahon will show that art and violence are closely allied:

> Eastward they are burning
> Witches and heretics
> In the boiling squares,
>
> Thousands have died since dawn
> In the service
> Of barbarous kings.

Snow in Raine's poem takes us both to Japanese poetry and to northern Irish poetry. In a sense, 'shovelled snow' is a tiny, even distressed haiku. That adjective 'boiling' reappears in the penultimate line of Raine's poem, carrying his suppressed fear of the fate that may overtake him when his plane touches down.

But, as I've noted, the anxiety here is also about the nature of art, because he is flying from a culture which can separate poetry from politics to a different society that doesn't make that separation. In 'The Last of the Fire Kings', a companion poem to 'The Snow Party', Mahon confronts this subject:

> Perfecting my cold dream
> Of a place out of time,
> A palace of porcelain.

Then he turns on this idea of the transcendental work of art:

> But the fire-loving
> People, rightly perhaps,
> Will not countenance this,
>
> Demanding that I inhabit,
> Like them, a world of
> Sirens, bin lids
> And bricked-up windows –
>
> Not to release them
> From the ancient curse
> But to die their creature and be thankful.

Mahon figures Irish history as 'the ancient curse', and Raine's image of the 'fault' in the linen sea is a version of this.

In Raine's poem, the shovelled snow is on one level a victim of violence, but because 'love' is scrambled in the adjective 'shovelled' I begin to see the bride in the snow – she, we assume, is dressed in white, but the bridegroom is nowhere to be seen. In a way, he's represented by the phallic shovel, or by the poet in the plane. The poet is excited at the prospect of being in Belfast, as well as fearful, and the bride symbolises this. Those white tea things are grouped on a dresser, an object that seems too solid for the context, almost Magritte-like in its surreal, disembodied definition. It sounds like an object from a Heaney poem, though there are no dressers there until the 'deal dresser' in 'The Harvest Bow' in Heaney's *Field Work*, which was published the same year, 1979, as *A Martian Sends a Postcard Home*, the volume in which 'Flying to Belfast' first appeared. But inside 'dresser' is 'dress', and it is this that produces the bride in a veil and the boiling curtains.

The bride is laughing 'at the sense of event', a phrase that draws on a famous journey poem, Larkin's 'The Whitsun Weddings':

> In parodies of fashion girls, heels and veils,
> All posed irresolutely, watching us go,
> As if out on the end of an event
> Waving goodbye.

The veils and the word 'event' appear in the poem, so does the sense of fatedness and irresolution, and the idea, in Larkin's phrase, of a 'happy funeral' and a 'religious wounding'.

Larkin is also present in the description of the fields as 'Intricate,/ neat and orderly'. This suggests that at least law and order is present in the pattern of hedged fields, because that word 'orderly' picks up Larkin's angry response to British withdrawal from Aden:

> Next year we are to bring the soldiers home
> For lack of money, and it is all right.
> Places they guarded, or kept orderly,
> Must guard themselves, and keep themselves orderly.

Larkin's 'Homage to a Government' attacks Harold Wilson's Labour Government for ending the British presence east of Suez. The word 'Intricate' describes the intricacy of the exposed radio set – its valves and wires and blob of solder. This could be the inside of a bomb, but it also suggests that the society that farms these fields is complicated like a net. In a sense, the word 'Intricate' contradicts 'neat and orderly'.

The word 'gleamed' echoes the closing image of Seamus Heaney's 'Sunlight', which opens *North*, published four years earlier in 1975:

and here is love
like a tinsmith's scoop
sunk past its gleam
in the meal bin.

Weapons gleam – famously in the night attack in the *Aeneid* – and when we look at 'solder' we might see a pun on 'soldier'. There is a play in 'wired up' on being extremely nervous, and, now I think of it, this is a subliminal sexual moment, which prepares us for the wedding image. The 'white tea things' are part of the poem's hard wiring because they pick up the tea image implicit in 'boiling', but the three monosyllables and the repeated *t*s also pick up 'Intricate', which stands out because of the capital 'I' and the word's position at the beginning of a sentence and at the end of the line. Inside it I hear 'trick' and see a trap. The word 'entered' is sexual, masculine, the cloud is female. The word 'nowhere' picks up the *o* in 'snow', but is a glance at a poem by Larkin which fuses sky, sex and height:

Rather than words comes the thought of high windows:
The sun-comprehending glass,
And beyond it, the deep blue air, that shows
Nothing, and is nowhere, and is endless.

Larkin's phrase 'Nothing, and is nowhere' survives in 'and were nowhere', the *no* being strong because of the echo of 'snow'. And 'windows' occurs in both Larkin and Raine. In a sense, the airplane is a flying high window. Another repetitive pattern takes the *b* in *Belfast* and echoes it in *boil bride boiling bedroom*. That image of the curtains blowing out of a bedroom window – the site of sexual initiation or an exploding bomb – perhaps echoes an image in MacNeice's 'Order to View':

A horse neighed
And all the curtains flew out of
The windows; the world was open.

These lines show that the moving curtains are also an image of aerial flight.

The phrase 'an empty house' may not have a particular source: Hardy in an elegy for his first wife speaks of the 'look of an empty room/ On returning thither,' and Eliot's Gerontion says 'I stiffen in a rented house'. An empty house is often a metaphor for the body, and as the *eh* in 'empty' is echoed by 'bedroom' we get something like 'deadroom'. Unlike MacNeice's image, this image isn't hopeful, because Raine is facing his anxious realisation that the private life cannot be isolated from history. Those curtains boiling out of the bedroom are an image of that uneasy outside/inside effect which is such a feature of Irish drama, where what in England would be perfectly protected living spaces are broken into or bring external reality inside because they look out on things happening outside. The empty house could represent the void at the heart of an idea of the private life separate from history, and so could the radio with its back ripped off, as though it has been violated.

The phrase 'empty house' does have some interesting reverberations: in his poem 'To Walter de la Mare', Eliot picks up on de la Mare's famous poem 'The Traveller', where the traveller knocks on the moonlit door of an empty house. Eliot says, 'when by chance/ An empty face peers from an empty house'. Eliot, following de la Mare, insists on the spookiness of the word. Yeats repeats the word four times in his 'The Stare's Nest', one of his sequence of Civil War poems:

> We had fed the heart on fantasies,
> The heart's grown brutal from the fare;
> More substance in our enmities
> Than in our love; O honey-bees,
> Come live in the empty house of the stare.

Eliot is fond of the adjective, and there is an 'empty house' in Mahon's 'Refusal to Mourn', with an angel 'In flight above the bed' occupied by the uncle who is near death. In poetry, an empty house is always ominous.

The bride in white glances back to the clouds and the Apple Charlotte, as the poet faces the fact that things are outside of his control, and symbolises this by identifying with the female. This idea of vulnerability is also there in the white tea things, the wedding presents, which are 'grouped on a dresser' rather like targets. This fragile crockery, which could receive boiled water, leads naturally to the veiled bride. The bride is only half-afraid of an empty house, so perhaps the poet shares her mixture of confident expectation and anxiety? He is going to be initiated into something. He knows that much as he might wish to, he cannot shut that bedroom window, which ends the poem ominously with a final *o* sound immediately after a *d*. Raine's poem is not overweighted by its poetic debts – it flies free of too-heavy allusion and succeeds, as it were, in transcending its several debts.

Jamie McKendrick ~ 'Apotheosis'

His bonce high-domed like a skep, the bee-man
holds forth on how to pick a bee up by its wings
which are strong enough – it stands to reason –
to bear the weight without harm to their hinges.
As though he were a banjo-player and the bee's wings
were a two-ply, fine abalone plectrum,
he demonstrates with a bumblebee on the windowframe
the exact grip between forefinger and thumb

but slips on the waxed oak floor, his arm outstretched,
neither tightening nor, regardless of his own fate,
loosening his hold on the bee one micro-notch.
I try to break his fall but move too late
for, with a dry hum, he streaks off out of reach
through the open window, still holding forth the bee.

The second word trips us – it's slightly daft slang for 'head' (from a nineteenth-century word for a big shooting marble). It has 'bounce' inside it, but a dry, curtailed, a trapped bounce that goes back on itself. The long *ee* in 'bee' breaks from this, but 'skep' is another trap: though it has 'skip' in it, it also has 'kept'. The three strong stresses at the start – 'bonce high-domed' – are broken out of by the skipping anapaest 'like a skep'. This noun, which means beehive, comes from the Old Norse for 'basket', and is somehow a dry, tight word. The spondee 'bee-man' acts like a barrier at the end of the line, a line which feels deliberated, enclosed, claustrophobic, with a hard bulge at the first spondee 'high-domed', a compound adjective which might be out of a book on neoclassical architecture. The *o*s in 'bonce' and 'domed' reflect each other, though they do not sound similar, and they set up the run of *o*s in the second line, as 'holds' picks up 'domed' and reverberates like an echo. The phrase 'holds forth' is usually used of tedious, boring or annoying speech, and we get a hint here that the bee-man may be all of these things. Also there's a joke in the link between the two physical actions of holding and picking up – the second action plays against the clichéd metaphor, and 'pick' takes a lot of stress because it echoes 'skep'.

Then the texture of the verse changes – the poet's ear is beginning to run with the *ih* in 'pick', but he's also interested in the guttural *k*. The *ih* travels to 'its wings', 'it', 'hinges'. The *k*, drawn down from 'skep', emphasises 'pick' in a tactile manner – the word stands out in the dead centre of the line. It is picked out. The last word rhymes, but not perfectly, with 'wings', and its extra, unstressed syllable, acts almost as a motor, making the word seem to flap like a wing. The *st* in 'strong' and 'stands' braces the line and passes their dental *t*s down to 'weight', which again has a bracing effect.

When 'reason' rhymes with 'bee-man', we also take it back to 'high-domed', to rational, neoclassical architecture like St Paul's Cathedral. This idea of the rational is the ground of the poem's surprise. But the rhythm is now starting to flex itself by drawing down the two spondees in the first line. We hear the two stresses on 'banjo', and we catch the tiny pause between the stresses, then another stress on 'play' follows, and very soon the spondaic 'bee's-wings', followed by 'two-ply, fine, abalone plectrum.' The word 'two' draws attention to the twoness of spondees, and then the rhythm shifts back into two iambic feet, 'He dem/onstrates,' before a pyrrhic foot of two unstressed syllables, 'with a', gives way to a cretic foot, 'bumblebee', another pyrrhic, 'on the', then a cretic, 'windowframe'. It's as though the cretics have crossed the unstressed syllables with the spondees to create a two-winged effect, which begins with the single wing of 'hinges'. The bee man has picked the bee up by its two wings folded together – the double thickness is necessary for the right degree of tension or twanginess.

The guttural *k* in 'skep' has passed to 'plectrum' and 'exact'; now it moves to 'waxed oak' as 'slips' echoes 'grip', but smoothed with a double susurrus. In the music of the poem, the *tch* sound in 'stretched' is picked up by 'notch' and 'reach', which assonate slightly but exactly with 'plectrum', while 'micro' picks up 'banjo'. The *ee* sounds in the sonnet culminate in the last line, which lacks an end-rhyme, so that the claustrophobia of the first line is triumphantly overcome. That 'open window' disposes of the fixed rationality of 'high-domed', while the final clause repeats his holding forth as a physical action which pays him back for boring his audience. By accident, the bee-man has become godlike, except his confident power has been transferred to the bee.

McKendrick was the first reviewer to point out the complexities of Paul Muldoon's rhyme schemes in *The Annals of Chile*, and it is clear from his seminal review that he has thought deeply about rhyme and form. If metrical, rhymed verse is the antithesis of free verse, a type of verse Frost compared to playing tennis without a net, 'Apotheosis' suggests that the tight formal structure of the sonnet's 'little room' (which is what the Italian word *sonetto* means) needs a *free/bee* spirit of anarchy that heads for the open and scorns bald, confident, boring formalism. This version of the Petrarchan, the tightest, sonnet form draws an anti-formalist element into itself which plays movement against stasis and introduces a spirit of comedy into the bee-man's serious discourse. The word 'baloney' flicks out of the richly voiced, knowing technical term 'abalone', which, with the banjo, might be taking us towards New Orleans, the Mississippi, black music and the Blues – far from high-domed rationality. It also frees up, through strong emphasis, the *o* in 'domed', drawing it out, arresting the rhythm at this point. Abalone is a particular type of shellfish prized for its mother-of-pearl, a univalve not a bivalve, a fact contradicted by the adjective 'two-ply' in the poem, which, as I say, enforces the theme of twoness. With this goes, perhaps, the theme of confidence and clumsiness, the latter quality prepared for by the 'bumble' in 'bumblebee', which leads to him slipping on a floor which may be waxed with beeswax. There is something heroic and slightly quixotic about him – he's not just a bald bore who talks too much.

Acknowledgements

I am grateful to my students for their help over more than thirty years in reading these poems. I am also grateful to Charlotte Brewer, Noah Comet, Eamonn Duffy, Roy Foster, Mina Gorji, Roger Lonsdale, Andrew MacNeillie, Alban Miles, Bernard O'Donoghue, Vidyan Ravinthiran, Lucy Reynolds, Jennifer Sykes, Emma Smith, Christopher Whalen and Duncan Wu. I owe a special debt to Jamie McKendrick for his help and advice. – T.P.

For permission to reprint copyright material the publishers gratefully acknowledge the following:

W. H. AUDEN: 'Musée des Beaux Arts' from *Selected Poems* (London: Faber and Faber, 1979), © The Estate of W. H. Auden, 1979, reprinted by permission of the publishers.
KEITH DOUGLAS: 'Canoe' from *The Complete Poems of Keith Douglas*, reprinted by permission of Faber and Faber Ltd and J. C. Hall.
ROBERT FROST: 'The Investment' and 'A Servant to Servants' from *The Poetry of Robert Frost* edited by Edward Connery Lathem, published by Jonathan Cape; reprinted by permission of the Random House Group Ltd.
SEAMUS HEANEY: 'Broagh' from *Wintering Out* (London: Faber and Faber, 1972), © Seamus Heaney, 1972, reprinted by permission of the publishers.
ZBIGNIEW HERBERT: 'Elegy of Fortinbras', © Zbigniew Herbert, 1961, from *Elegy for the Departure* by Zbigniew Herbert, translation by John and Bogdana Carpenter; copyright © Zbigniew Herbert, 1999; translation copyright © 1999 by John Carpenter and Bogdana Carpenter. Reprinted by permission of HarperCollins Publishers.

TED HUGHES: 'Thistles' from *Wodwo* (London: Faber and Faber, 1973), © The Estate of Ted Hughes, 1973, reprinted by permission of the publishers.
PATRICK KAVANAGH: 'Kerr's Ass' is reprinted from *Collected Poems*, edited by Antoinette Quinn (Allen Lane, 2004), by kind permission of the Trustees of the Estate of the late Katherine B. Kavanagh, through the Jonathan Williams Literary Agency.
PHILIP LARKIN: 'Cut Grass' from *High Windows* (London: Faber and Faber, 1979), © The Estate of Philip Larkin, 1979, reprinted by permission of the publishers.
ROBERT LOWELL: 'Sailing Home from Rapallo' from *Collected Poems* by Robert Lowell, copyright © 2003 by Harriet Lowell and Sheridan Lowell; reprinted by permission of Farrar, Straus and Giroux, LLC.
JAMIE MCKENDRICK: 'Apotheosis' from *Ink Stone* (London: Faber and Faber, 2003) © Jamie McKendrick, 2003, reprinted by permission of the publishers.
LOUIS MACNEICE: 'Order to View' © Louis MacNeice, reprinted by permission of David Higham Associates.
DEREK MAHON: 'A Disused Shed in Co. Wexford' reprinted by kind permission of the author and The Gallery Press, Loughcrew, Oldcastle, County Meath, Ireland, from *Collected Poems* (1999).
john montague: 'All Legendary Obstacles' reprinted by kind permission of the author and The Gallery Press, Loughcrew, Oldcastle, County Meath, Ireland, from *Collected Poems* (1995).
PAUL MULDOON: 'Quoof' from *Quoof* (London: Faber and Faber, 1983) © Paul Muldoon, 1983, reprinted by permission of the publishers.
CRAIG RAINE: 'Flying to Belfast' from *The Onion, Memory*, published by Pan Macmillan, copyright © Craig Raine, 1978.
W. B. YEATS: 'Sailing to Byzantium' and 'In Memory of Eva Gore-Booth and Con Markiewicz' reproduced by kind permission of A. P. Watt Ltd on behalf of Gráinne Yeats.